Mapping Our World

Asia

by
Fran Sammis

***B*ENCHMARK *B*OOKS**

MARSHALL CAVENDISH
NEW YORK

Marshall Cavendish Corporation
99 White Plains Road
Tarrytown, New York 10591-9001

© Marshall Cavendish Corporation 1999

Series created by Blackbirch Graphics, Inc.

Photo Credits
Page 13: ©Bill O'Connor/Peter Arnold, Inc.; page 18: ©Fritz Polking/Peter Arnold, Inc.; page 19: © Gerard Lacz/Peter Arnold, Inc. (tapir) and ©Roland Seitre/Peter Arnold, Inc. (dragon); page 23: ©Cliff Hollenbeck/International Stock; pages 34 and 58: © Michael Von Ruber/International Stock; pages 37 and 38: © North Wind Pictures; page 45: ©Floyd Holdman/International Stock; page 54: ©Jeff Greenberg/ Peter Arnold, Inc.; page 56: ©Chad Ehlers/International Stock.

Printed in Hong Kong

Library of Congress Cataloging-in-Publication Data

Sammis, Fran.
   Asia / by Fran Sammis
      p.   cm. — (Mapping our world)
   Includes bibliographical references (p. 63) and index.
   Summary: Text, photographs, and maps introduce information about the climate, regions, people, cultures, animals, plants, resources, politics, and religions of Asia.
   ISBN 0-7614-0371-X
   1. Cartography—Asia—Juvenile literature. [1. Cartography—Asia 2. Asia—Maps.] I. Title. II. Series: Sammis, Fran. Mapping our world.
   GA1081.S36   1998
   912.5—dc21   98-16516
                                                                    CIP
                                                                    AC

Contents

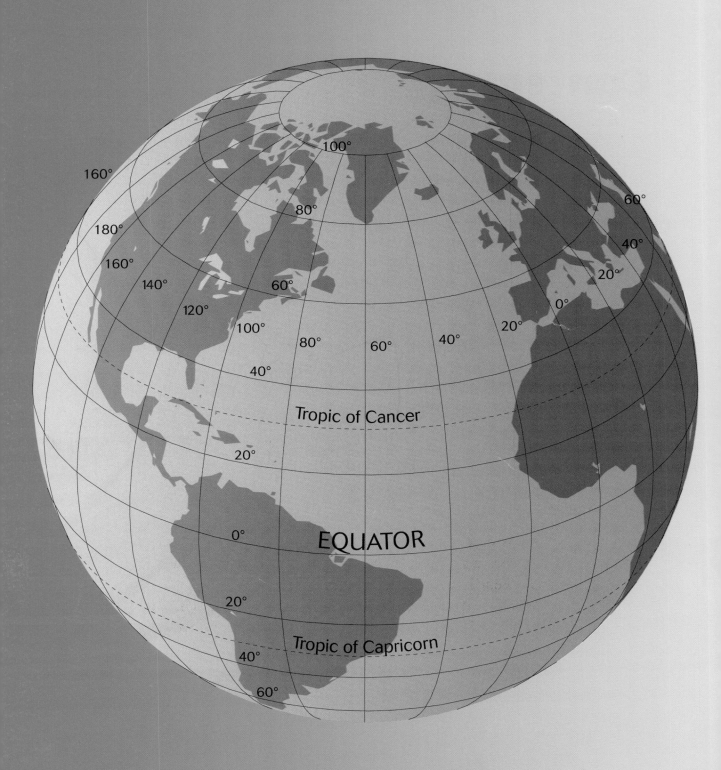

Tropic of Cancer

EQUATOR

Tropic of Capricorn

The Importance of Maps

As tools for understanding and navigating the world around us, maps are an essential resource. Maps provide us with a representation of a place, drawn or printed on a flat surface. The place that is shown may be as vast as the solar system or as small as a neighborhood park. What we learn about the place depends on the kind of map we are using.

Kinds of Maps

Physical maps show what the land itself looks like. These maps can be used to locate and identify natural geographic features such as mountains, bodies of water, deserts, and forests.

Distribution maps show where something can be found. There are two kinds of distribution maps. One shows the range or area a feature covers, such as a map showing where grizzly bears live or where hardwood forests grow.

The second kind of distribution map shows the density of a feature. That is, how much or how little of the feature is present. These maps allow us to see patterns in the way a feature is distributed. Rainfall and population maps are two examples of this kind of distribution map.

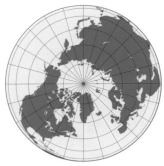

Globular

Mercator

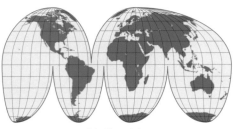

Mollweide

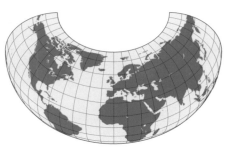

Armadillo

Political maps show us how an area is divided into countries, states, provinces, or other units. They also show where cities and towns are located. Major highways and transportation routes are also included on some kinds of political maps.

Movement maps help us find our way around. They can be road maps, street maps, and public transportation maps. Special movement maps called "charts" are used by airplane or boat pilots to navigate through air or on water.

Why Maps Are Important

Many people depend on maps to do their jobs. A geologist, for example, uses maps of Earth's structure to locate natural resources such as coal or petroleum. A transportation planner will use population maps to determine where new roads may need to be built.

A map can tell us how big a place is, where one place is in relation to another, what a place was like in the past, and what it's like now. Maps help us understand and move through our own part of the world and the rest of the world, too. Some maps even help us move through our solar system and universe!

Terms to Know

Maps are created and designed by incorporating many different elements and accepted cartographic (mapmaking) techniques. Often, maps showing the exact same area will differ from one another, depending upon the choice or critical elements, such as scale and projection. Following is a brief listing of some key mapmaking terms.

Projection. A projection is a way to represent the round Earth on a flat surface. There are a number of different ways to project, or transfer, round-Earth information to a flat surface, though each method results in some distortion. That is, areas may appear larger or smaller than they really are—or closer or farther apart. The maps on page 6 show a few varieties of projections.

Latitude. Lines of latitude, or parallels, run parallel to the equator (the imaginary center of Earth's circumference) and are used to locate points north and south of the equator. The equator is 0 degrees latitude, the north pole is 90 degrees north latitude, and the south pole is 90 degrees south latitude.

Longitude. Lines of longitude, or meridians, run at right angles to the equator and meet at the north and south poles. Lines of longitude are used to locate points east and west of the prime meridian.

Prime meridian. An imaginary line that runs through Greenwich, England; considered 0 degrees longitude. Lines to the west of the prime meridian go halfway around the world to 180 degrees west longitude; lines to the east go to 180 degrees east longitude.

Hemisphere. A half circle. Dividing the world in half from pole to pole along the prime meridian gives you the eastern and western hemispheres. Dividing the world in half at the equator gives you the northern and southern hemispheres.

Scale. The relationship of distance on a map to the actual distance on the ground. Scale can be expressed in three ways:

1. As a ratio—1:63,360 (one inch equals 63,360 inches)
2. Verbally—one inch equals one mile
3. Graphically— [1 mi.]

Because 63,360 inches equal one mile, these scales give the same information: one map-inch equals one mile on the ground.

Large-scale maps show a small area, such as a city park, in great detail. Small-scale maps show a large area, such as an entire continent, in much less detail, and on a much smaller scale.

The Art and Process of Mapmaking

Maps have been made for thousands of years. Early maps, based on first-hand exploration, were some of the most accurate tools of their

◀◀ *Opposite: The maps shown here are just four of the many different projections in which the world can be displayed.*

225 million years ago

1

180 million years ago

2

65 million years ago

3

present day

4

time. Others, based on guesses about what an area was like, were often very beautiful, but were not especially accurate.

As technology—such as photography and flight—evolved, cartographers (mapmakers) were able not only to map most of Earth in detail, they were also able to make maps of our solar system.

To make a map today, cartographers first determine what a map is to show and who is most likely to use it. Then, they assemble the information they will need for the map, which can come from many different kinds of experts—such as meteorologists, geologists, and surveyors—as well as from aerial photography or satellite feedback.

Mapping a Changing Earth

If you traced around all the land masses shown on a world map, then cut them out and put them together like a jigsaw puzzle, the result would look something like map 1 at the top of this page. Scientists think this is how Earth looked about 225 million years ago.

Over time, this single continent, Pangaea (Pan–JEE–uh), slowly broke apart into two land masses called Laurasia and Gondwanaland (map 2). Maps 3 and 4 show how the land masses continued to break up and drift apart over millions of years, until the continents assumed the shapes and positions we recognize today. Earth has not, however, finished changing.

Scientists have established that Earth's surface is made up of sections called tectonic plates. These rigid plates, shown in the map on page 9, are in

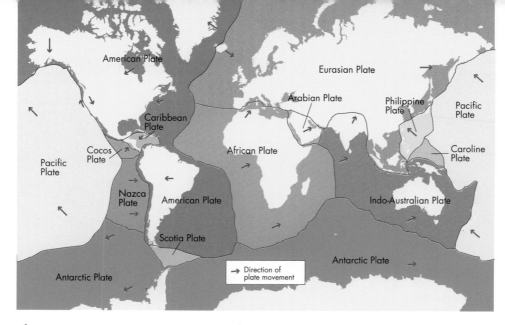

 Left: The tectonic plates that lie beneath Earth's surface are in a slow but constant motion.

◀◀ *Opposite:* The continents of our planet were once clumped together but have spread apart over millions of years in what is called continental drift.

slow, constant motion, moving from 1/4 to 1 inch a year. As they move, they take the continents and sea floors with them. Sometimes, their movements cause disasters, such as earthquakes and volcanic activity.

After many more millions of years have passed, our Earth's continents will again look very different from what we know today.

Reading a Map

In order for a map to be useful, it must be the right kind of map for the job. A small-scale map of Illinois would not help you find your way around Chicago; for that, you would need a large-scale map of the city. A physical map of North America would not tell you where most of the people live; you would need a distribution map that shows population.

Once you have found the right map, you will need to refer to the map legend, or key, to be sure you are interpreting the map's information correctly. Depending on the type of map, the legend tells the scale used for the map, and notes the meaning of any symbols and colors used.

In their most basic form, maps function as place finders. They show us where places are, and we use these maps to keep from getting lost. But as you have begun to see, maps can tell us much more about our world than simply where places are located. Just how much more, you'll discover in the chapters ahead.

Physical Map

Arctic Ocean

RUSSIA
(partial)

Caspian Sea

Aral
Sea

Yenisey

Ob

Lena

Bering
Sea

KAZAKHSTAN
(partial)

UZBEKISTAN

TURKMENISTAN

TAJIKISTAN

AFGHANISTAN

KYRGYZSTAN

Lake Balkash

Lake
Baikal

Amur

MONGOLIA

Sea of
Japan

JAPAN

KARAKORAM RANGE
Godwin
Austen

Indus

Huang Ho

N. KOREA

S. KOREA

PAKISTAN

Ganges

H I M A L A Y A S

CHINA

Arabian
Sea

INDIA

NEPAL

Mt. Everest

Brahmaputra

Yangtze

Irawaddy

Pacific
Ocean

BHUTAN

BANGLADESH

Bay of
Bengal

MYANMAR

Mekong

South
China
Sea

TAIWAN

SRI LANKA

THAILAND

LAOS

PHILIPPINES

VIETNAM

CAMBODIA

BRUNEI

MALAYSIA

SINGAPORE

Indian
Ocean

INDONESIA

Key

*Feet (meters)
above sea level*

■	20 (6)
■	1,000 (305)
■	5,000 (1,524)
■	10,000 (3,048)

Mapping Natural Zones and Regions

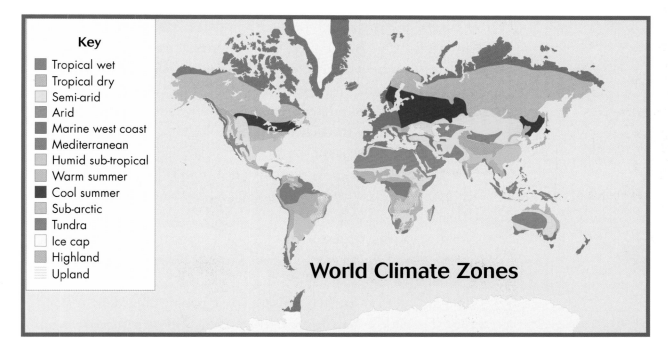

Key
- Tropical wet
- Tropical dry
- Semi-arid
- Arid
- Marine west coast
- Mediterranean
- Humid sub-tropical
- Warm summer
- Cool summer
- Sub-arctic
- Tundra
- Ice cap
- Highland
- Upland

World Climate Zones

Asia is a land of extremes. It is the largest of the continents—almost a third of all the land on Earth is part of Asia. It stretches almost 5,400 miles (8, 690 kilometers) from north to south, and about 4,500 miles (7,200 kilometers) at its greatest east–west point. The climate ranges from the world's coldest to the hottest. The highest mountain and deepest freshwater lake are located in Asia, and the largest lake is

▲ *Above: Asia and North America both have a wide range of climates.*

◀◀ *Opposite: The highest mountains in the world are in Asia's Karakoram and Himalaya mountain ranges.*

partly in Asia. Finally, Asia has the most people of any continent, as well as the world's most populated city and country.

Asia's northernmost boundary lies in the Arctic Circle, and its southernmost boundary lies below the equator. The northern half of the Asian continent lies between the Ural Mountains in the west and the Pacific Ocean in the east. The southern half extends from the Mediterranean and Red Seas in the west to the Pacific Ocean.

Asia has five main regions:

- South Asia includes India, Pakistan, Afghanistan, Nepal, Bhutan, Bangladesh, and Sri Lanka.
- Southeast Asia includes the entire peninsula east of India and south of China, and the islands of the Philippines, Malaysia, Brunei, and Indonesia. One of the islands of Indonesia, called New Guinea, spans two continents. The western half of the island is called Irian Jaya. It is considered to be part of Asia. The eastern half, Papua New Guinea, is considered to be part of the continent of Australia.
- East Asia takes up the eastern portion of China, as well as North Korea, South Korea, and Japan.
- Central Asia includes Turkmenistan, Uzbekistan, Tajikistan, Kyrgyzstan, Kazakhstan, Mongolia, and the western portion of China.
- North Asia, the largest section, covers more than a third of the continent and is occupied by Asian Russia. This area is also known as Siberia.

In addition to these five regions, some people consider the countries of the Middle East to be part of Asia. This area is covered in the volume of *Mapping Our World* called *Europe and the Middle East*, and the region's countries and features are discussed there. Papua New Guinea, in Indonesia, will be included in the volume called *Australia and the South Pacific*.

To learn about what Asia is like, you might start by referring to maps that show its physical features (topography), climate, land use, and other natural characteristics.

Asia's Topography

Mountains, rocky plateaus, deserts, and plains cover much of Asia. If you look at the physical map on page 10, you'll notice that among the most striking physical features of Asia are its large mountain ranges. The area where Afghanistan, Pakistan, Tajikistan, and China come together is where many of the major mountain chains begin.

One of the most well known, the Himalaya, runs along the south-western border of China. There, on the Nepal-China border, is where you'll find Mount Everest, the highest mountain in the world at 29,028 feet (8,848 meters) above sea level. It was not until 1849 that British surveyors determined that Mount Everest was the world's tallest mountain. They named it in honor of George Everest, a surveyor who worked for more than 20 years to help map the whole of India, from its southernmost point to the base of the Himalayas in the north.

North of the Himalayas is another important mountain range, the Karakoram Range. The world's second-highest mountain, Godwin Austen, is found there. In fact, the 35 highest mountains in the world are located in either the Himalaya or Karakoram Ranges. Other major mountain ranges extend west into Afghanistan, and east and northeast into China and Mongolia.

▼ *Below:* Mount Everest is the world's tallest mountain. Its peak, in the center, is 29,028 feet (8,848 meters) above sea level.

The huge mountain plateau that makes up southwestern China, colored dark brown, is easy to spot on the physical map. This was not always the case! Europeans had not mapped this area of Asia until well into the 1800s. The difficult terrain had discouraged them from exploring and mapping the region.

The mountain systems of Central Asia are the source for many important Asian rivers that have created valuable agricultural land and provided key transportation routes. Among these major rivers are the Indus in Pakistan, the Ganges in India, and the Brahmaputra in Bangladesh. Asia's longest river, at 3,400 miles (5,472 kilometers), is the Yangtze, located in China. The major rivers of North Asia—the Ob, Yenisey, Lena, and Amur—don't originate in the central mountains.

The Caspian Sea, which is actually the world's largest lake, lies partly in Asia on the western border of Kazakhstan and Turkmenistan, and partly in Europe. The Caspian Sea is considered a lake because it is surrounded by land. It received its misleading name—*Mare Caspium*—from the Romans. They called it a sea (*mare*) because it contains saltwater, not freshwater. Lake Baikal, in Russia, is the world's deepest freshwater lake at a depth of 5,712 feet (1,741 meters).

Deserts are found throughout Asia. The Thar Desert lies on both sides of the border between Pakistan and India. A large band of desert and semi-desert land spreads from Kazakhstan into west and north-west China, and on through Mongolia. The Gobi Desert in southern Mongolia is one of the world's largest deserts. It is famous for enormous dinosaur fossils that have been found there. These fossils have convinced scientists that the Gobi was once a humid region with many plants.

Major plains areas are found in northern India, eastern China, and southwestern Russia.

Climate and Weather

Asia's physical traits are affected by its climate. Climate and weather are not the same thing. Weather is short-lived; it changes from day to day. Climate is the average characteristics of the weather in a given place over a period of time. Although climates can change, they do so much more slowly than weather—over many years, rather than days.

Meteorologists use a variety of high-tech methods to gather the information that allows them to analyze and predict the weather. Among those methods are sophisticated ways of viewing and mapping the world.

Analyzing and Predicting Weather

The major elements that are used to describe the weather and categorize climate are: temperature, precipitation, humidity, amount of sunshine, wind, and air pressure.

Manned and unmanned weather stations on land and at sea, weather balloons, airplanes, and satellites are all used in gathering weather information for analysis. Radar, cameras, and thermal infrared sensors monitor and record the weather conditions.

The information from these sources is sent to weather centers throughout the world by means of a worldwide satellite system, called the Global Telecommunications System (GTS). The information is fed into computers that record and analyze the data, which can then be compiled into highly detailed and informative maps. The GTS also allows weather centers to share their data.

By studying global weather patterns over a long time, climatologists can map climatic regions—areas that have similar climates. The world climate zones map on page 11 is just one example of this kind of map.

Asia's Climate

Stretching from the tundra in the north to the tropics in the south, Asia covers a wide range of climates, as you can see by the map on page 16.

- The tundra regions (shown in dark purple) are always cold, and have little precipitation. There is a summer season, but it is very

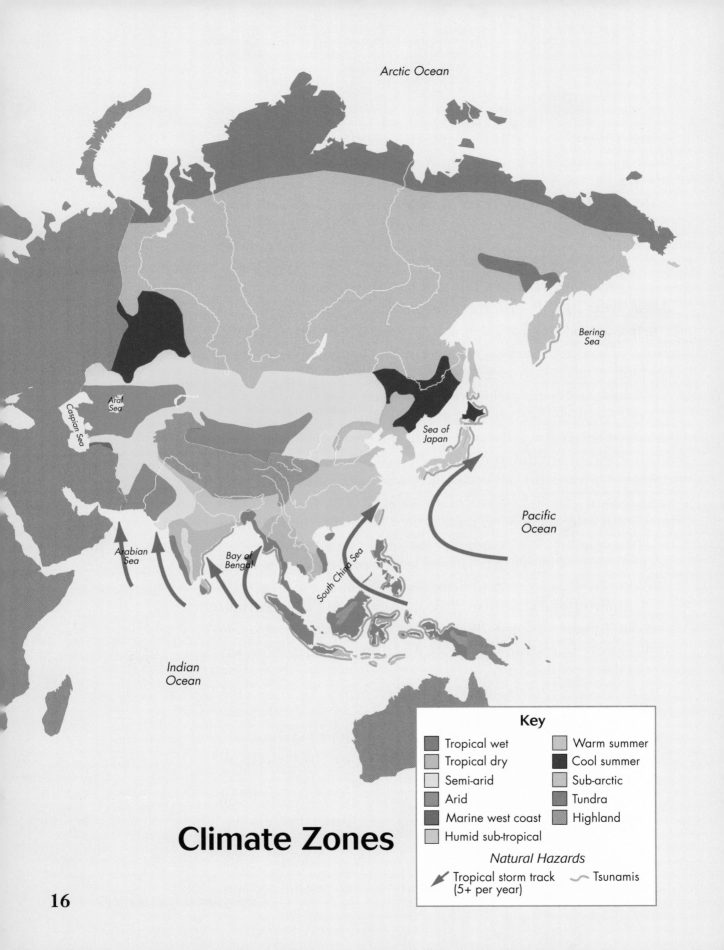

Climate Zones

Arctic Ocean

Bering Sea

Pacific Ocean

Sea of Japan

Aral Sea

Caspian Sea

Arabian Sea

Bay of Bengal

South China Sea

Indian Ocean

Key

- Tropical wet
- Tropical dry
- Semi-arid
- Arid
- Marine west coast
- Humid sub-tropical
- Warm summer
- Cool summer
- Sub-arctic
- Tundra
- Highland

Natural Hazards

- ↗ Tropical storm track (5+ per year)
- ∼ Tsunamis

short and chilly. This is the only time of year that the ground isn't frozen and, even then, only the topmost layer thaws.

- The sub-arctic climate (light purple) features a short, cool summer and a long, cold winter. Light to moderate precipitation occurs mainly in the summer. Winter temperatures are among the lowest in the world. They average -60 degrees Fahrenheit (-51 degrees Celsius) in the month of January.

- A moist, continental climate is characteristic of southwestern and southeastern Russia and northern Japan. This area, shown in dark blue on the climate map, features cool summers and cold winters. Precipitation is moderate year-round.

- The climate across the middle of Asia and in part of the southwest is either semi-arid (gold) or arid (red). The semi-arid areas receive only about 10 to 15 inches of precipitation a year, while the arid areas receive even less. Temperatures can fluctuate widely in these areas. For example, in the Gobi Desert, in Central Asia, summer temperatures reach 100 degrees Fahrenheit (38 degrees Celsius). In winter, they fall as low as -30 degrees Fahrenheit (-34 degrees Celsius).

- Highland regions (colored olive) have a climate that is affected by their altitude. Mountains or high hills generally keep the land cooler and wetter than the surrounding areas.
  Compare the climate map with the physical map. You can see that the large highland climate region centered in southern Asia is associated with the continent's mountain chains and plateaus. Southern Japan also experiences a highland climate.

- A humid sub-tropical climate is typical of southeastern and southern China. China's primary agricultural lands are located in this region, which is marked by warm to hot summers, cool winters, and moderate precipitation all year.

- In most of the South and Southeast mainland Asia, the climate is tropical dry. Here, winds called monsoons create both wet and dry seasons. During the wet season—which extends from spring to early fall—rainfall is heavy.

◀◀ *Opposite: About half of Asia experiences a sub-arctic climate, with long, cold winters.*

• In some regions of the South and Southeast on the mainland and on the islands of Southeast Asia, rainfall is heavy throughout the year. This is the tropical wet region (colored dark green) where rain forests are located.

Animals and Plants

Because Asia has such a wide variety of climate regions, the continent is home to many different animals and plants. The cold tundra areas support mosses, lichens, and some low-growing shrubs. Summer brings flowering plants. Tundra vegetation tends to grow close to the ground and, if there are flowers, the blossoms are small. Among the animals that make their home in the area are Arctic foxes and hares, lemmings, and reindeer.

South of the tundra, the sub-arctic region of Asia, is covered with pine and fir trees. Because its climate is less severe, the region has more animal species than the tundra. Reindeer live there, as do many valuable fur-bearing animals such as sable, lynx, and ermine. In addition, there are bears, elk, and wolves.

Semi-arid areas are home to various kinds of antelope and rodents. The plains found there are covered with grasses that provide food for herds of domesticated cattle, sheep, horses, and goats.

Yaks, with their long, shaggy fur, live in the Himalayas. People ride them and use them to work the land. Thick-furred snow leopards and wild sheep also make their home in the colder regions of mainland Asia. In the chilly mountain forests of Japan's highlands, you'll find macaques. Like other cold-climate animals, these monkeys have thick, shaggy fur that keep them warm.

▼ *Below:* This Japanese macaque has thick fur to protect it against the cold climate of Japan's highlands.

Animals that can survive with little water—such as gerbils, jerboas, and camels—make their home in the arid desert regions of Asia. Water-storing succulents, or cactus, and drought-tolerant thorn plants are also found there.

Tropical South and Southeast Asia have an amazing variety of animals and plants. Mangrove trees grow in coastal swamps, and hundreds of different tree species crowd the rain forests. Among the valuable trees of this region are teak—used for fine furniture—and rubber trees. Many exotic flowers are found there, including a variety of orchids and the world's largest flower, which is called *Rafflesia arnoldi*. It is nearly 3 feet (1 meter) across and weighs about 15 pounds. However, the most unusual thing about it is not its size but its scent—it smells like rotting meat!

Among the many animals found in the tropics are tigers, elephants, leopards, crocodiles, orangutans, rhinoceros, and tapirs—pig-like animals with long snouts. The beautiful peacock with its bright, trailing tail is the national bird of India. The king cobra—the longest poisonous snake in the world at 18 feet (5 meters)—is one of the many snakes that live in this warm, moist climate.

Of all the different kinds of bears that live throughout Asia, the most famous is the giant panda, which is found only in southwestern China. The Komodo dragon of Indonesia is another animal unique to Asia. This huge lizard is a relative of the ancient meat-eating dinosaurs. A Komodo dragon can grow to 10 feet (3 meters) in length and weigh more than 300 pounds (136 kilograms).

▲ ◀ *Above left:* Tapirs, such as this adult and its young, are at home in the tropics.

▲ ▶ *Above right:* A Komodo dragon stands in the surf in Indonesia.

How Climate and Topography Affect People

As we have seen, climate greatly affects plant and animal life. Of course, a region's climate and topography can affect many aspects of human life as well. Among them:

Population distribution. More people tend to settle in areas that have a mild or moderate climate, adequate rainfall, and fairly level, open land. Population will be less densely distributed in regions that are mountainous or thickly forested, and in regions with climates that are very cold or dry. You can see this connection if you compare the world climate zones map on page 11 in this chapter with the world population density map on page 33 in Chapter 2.

How people live and work. The type of housing people live in, the clothes they wear, and the kind of work they do, all depend in part on the climate of their region. The physical structure of the land also can affect what work people do. For example, large-scale farming is an option in plains areas, but not in mountain regions.

Agriculture. To a large extent, climate dictates what crops can or can't be successfully grown in an area. Using technology, such as artificial irrigation or greenhouses, can change the impact of weather and climate to a degree. However, agriculture is most successful when crops are naturally suited to the area in which they are grown.

Transportation. An area's climate and topography can dictate which forms of transportation are used there. For example, dogsleds are an obvious choice in arctic areas, while camels or elephants are well suited to travel in hot, arid conditions. More roads and railroads will be built in areas that have a level terrain, as opposed to mountainous areas.

Economy. Some areas, such as deserts, have little or no natural resources. These areas have a climate or topography that doesn't allow for extensive agriculture or a developed transportation system. Such harsh regions will most likely be poorer than areas that can support industry, large-scale agriculture, or other means of making a living and engaging in trade.

▶▶ *Opposite: Asia's most important grain crops are rice and wheat.*

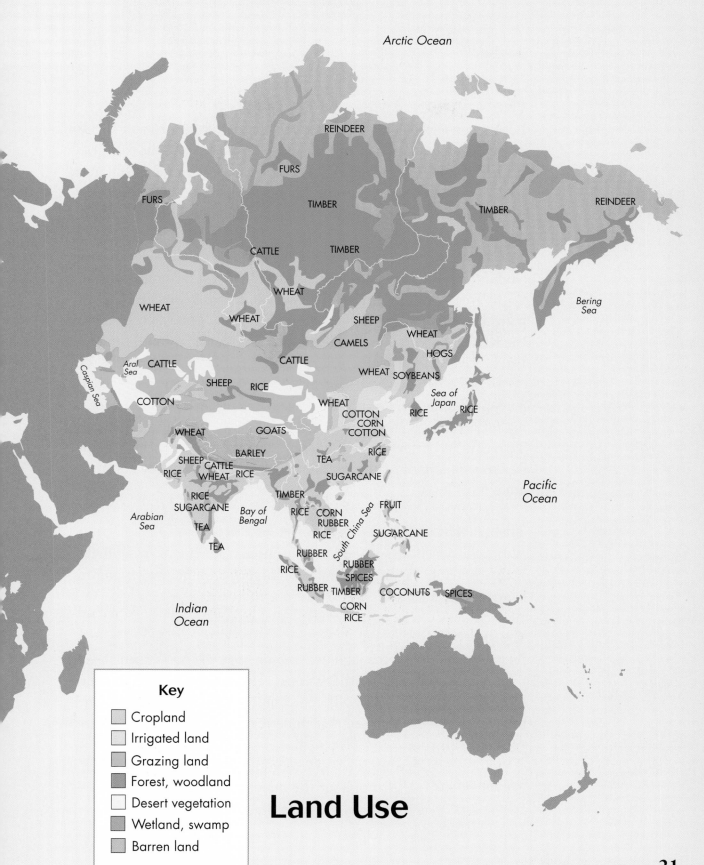

Arctic Ocean

REINDEER

FURS

TIMBER

FURS

TIMBER

REINDEER

CATTLE

TIMBER

Bering Sea

WHEAT

SHEEP

WHEAT

WHEAT

WHEAT

CAMELS

Aral Sea CATTLE

CATTLE

WHEAT

SOYBEANS

HOGS

Caspian Sea

SHEEP

RICE

WHEAT

Sea of Japan

COTTON

WHEAT

COTTON
CORN
COTTON

RICE

RICE

WHEAT

GOATS

RICE

TEA

SHEEP CATTLE

BARLEY

SUGARCANE

Pacific Ocean

RICE

WHEAT

RICE

RICE

FRUIT

RICE
SUGARCANE

TIMBER

RICE CORN
RUBBER

South China Sea

Arabian Sea

TEA

Bay of Bengal

RICE

SUGARCANE

TEA

RUBBER

RUBBER
SPICES

RUBBER

RICE

RUBBER TIMBER

COCONUTS

SPICES

Indian Ocean

CORN
RICE

Key

- Cropland
- Irrigated land
- Grazing land
- Forest, woodland
- Desert vegetation
- Wetland, swamp
- Barren land

Land Use

The Land of Asia and Its People

Look again at the climate and physical maps on pages 16 and 10. You might conclude that most of Asia's climate and much of its topography are unsuitable for agriculture. There is not enough rainfall in many areas, and there is not a great deal of open, level land. However, agriculture is Asia's most important economic activity. The land use map on page 21 shows that crops are grown in much of the arid and semi-arid climate regions, as well as in hilly areas. People have adapted the land in two different ways to make it suitable for farming.

In areas with little rainfall, dams and canals have been built to provide water for artificial irrigation systems. One such system is the Kara Kum Canal in Turkmenistan. The canal taps into the Amu Darya River and provides water for huge cotton plantations.

In places where there is little level ground for planting, such as parts of Taiwan and Japan, farmers gain extra growing room by forming terraced fields shaped like steps that "climb" up the steep hillsides. Terracing and irrigation are important because Asia's enormous population—the largest of any continent—demands an equally enormous amount of food.

The Land of Asia and the Economy

Although agriculture is the major economic activity of Asia, the land is also valuable for the minerals it contains, and the forests and fur-bearing animals it supports.

Crops

As you can see from the land use map on page 21, Asia's farmlands lie mainly in South and Southeast Asia, eastern China, and the southwestern portion of Russia. If you compare this map with the climate map on page 16, you'll see that these regions have the most favorable growing climates.

Wheat and rice are the two major grain crops of Asia. Wheat is grown extensively throughout the main cropland regions. Rice—

which thrives in warm, wet climates—is grown primarily in southern areas. Russia and China are the world's leading wheat producers, and China and India produce the most rice.

Asia is the main source of tea and rubber worldwide. Major tea-growing countries include China and Sri Lanka. Large quantities of rubber are produced by Indonesia, Malaysia, and Thailand.

India is a leading world producer of sugarcane, which is also grown in China and the Philippines. Much of the world's supply of cotton comes from Asia. Cotton is grown in many different areas, as you can see from the land use map. The leading producers are China and the former Soviet republics in western Asia.

Other crops grown on the continent include coconuts and spices in Indonesia, fruit in the Philippines, and soybeans in northeastern China.

Timber

Wood and wood products are economically important in Russia, which has huge stands of timber in the north, as the land use map shows. Timber is also a major resource in Myanmar (formerly Burma) and throughout Indonesia.

Fur

Valuable fur-bearing animals—including ermine, lynx, and sable—are found in North Asia. In Uzbekistan, Karakul sheep are raised especially for their wool, which is used worldwide for making coats.

In western China and northern India, cashmere goats are raised for their ultra-soft mohair coats, which are sheared and made into sweaters and other garments.

Mineral Resources

A variety of mineral resources are found in Asia. If you look at the mineral resources map on the opposite page, you'll notice that these resources are concentrated most heavily in the southern and southeastern portions of the continent. Additional deposits are found in northern and far western Asia.

Coal is one of Asia's primary mineral products. It is discussed below under the heading Energy Production and Consumption. Major deposits of gold are also found in North Asia. Iron ore is found extensively in China and India, and Malaysia has the world's largest tin deposits. Extensive deposits of manganese are found in India and southern China. Asia is also rich in tungsten; China has more than half the world's supply. Copper deposits are found in western Asia, China, Indonesia, and the Philippines. Nickel is also found in Indonesia and in the Philippines, where there are major deposits of chromite.

Energy Production and Consumption

A look at the energy production map on page 26 shows that Asia has extensive energy resources in the southern half of the continent. Here you will find China's coal fields and oil basins and fields, and the extensive natural gas fields of Turkmenistan and Pakistan. Natural gas is also concentrated along the southern coasts of the mainland and in Malaysia, Indonesia, and Japan. Malaysia and Indonesia also have extensive oil deposits.

In northern Asia, or Siberia, coal fields contribute the most to energy production. Russia would like to use more of its energy resources in Siberia. The difficulty is getting them out of the frozen ground and transporting them. In addition to coal, there are some gas fields and oil in Siberia, primarily in the west.

▶▶ *Opposite:* Asia's minerals are concentrated heavily along the southern coast.

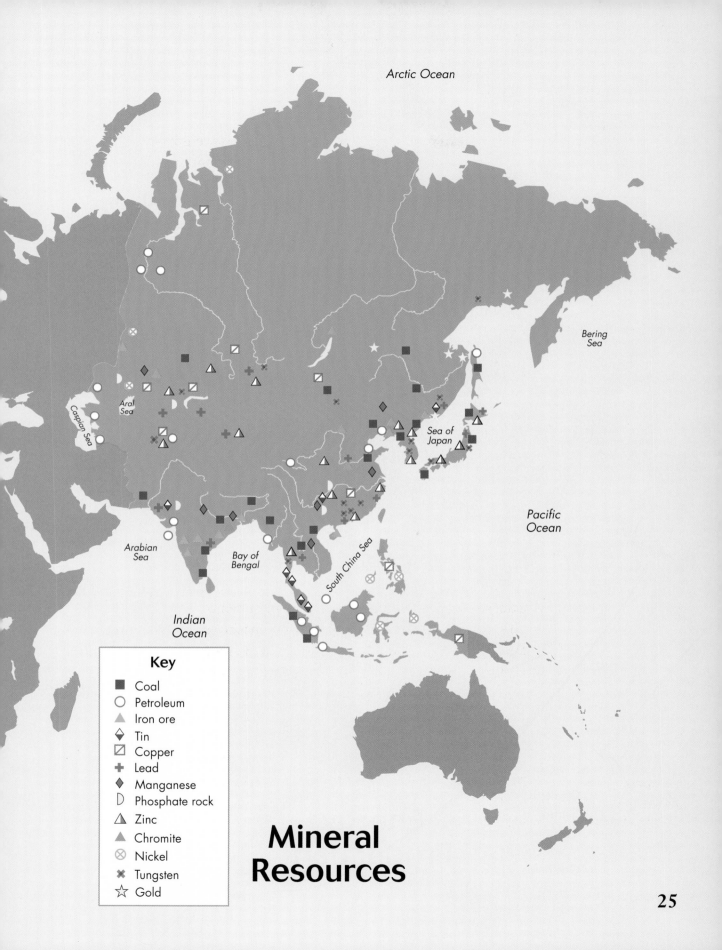

Arctic Ocean

Bering Sea

Pacific Ocean

Sea of Japan

South China Sea

Bay of Bengal

Indian Ocean

Arabian Sea

Caspian Sea

Aral Sea

Key

- ■ Coal
- ○ Petroleum
- ▲ Iron ore
- ◆ Tin
- ▨ Copper
- ✛ Lead
- ◆ Manganese
- ⋗ Phosphate rock
- △ Zinc
- ▲ Chromite
- ⊗ Nickel
- ✕ Tungsten
- ☆ Gold

Mineral Resources

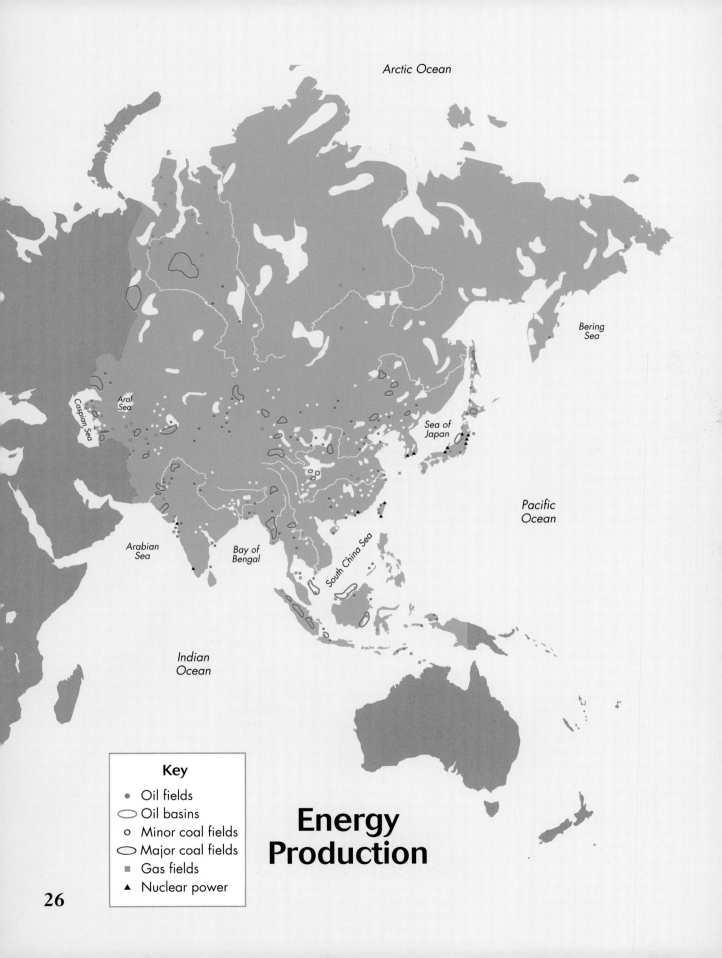

Arctic Ocean

Bering
Sea

Caspian Sea

Aral
Sea

Sea of
Japan

Pacific
Ocean

Arabian
Sea

Bay of
Bengal

South China Sea

Indian
Ocean

Energy Production

Key

- • Oil fields
- ⬭ Oil basins
- ○ Minor coal fields
- ⬯ Major coal fields
- ◼ Gas fields
- ▲ Nuclear power

The areas that consume the most energy per person (see the map below) are northern and western Asia. Mining, oil and gas production, and heating account in large part for the heavy energy consumption in this region. To see how Asia compares to the rest of the world in energy production and consumption, see the maps on page 28.

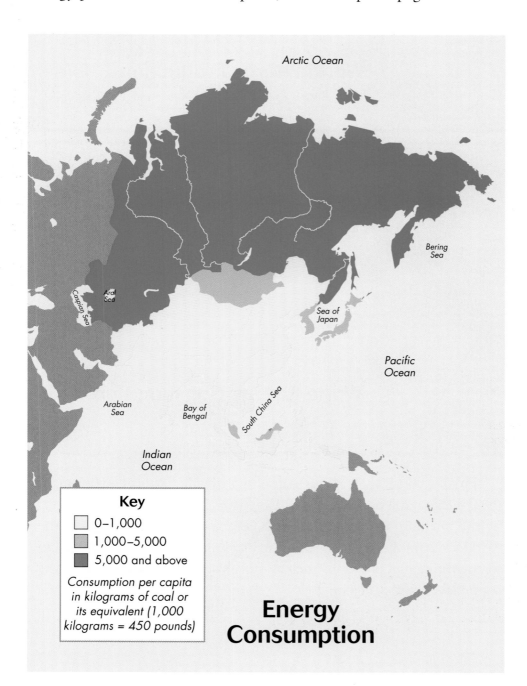

◀ **Left:** *The largest coal fields in Asia are found in the north.*

◀◀ **Opposite:** *If you compare this map with the climate map on page 16, you will notice that the coldest regions of Asia have the highest energy consumption per person.*

Arctic Ocean

Bering Sea

Caspian Sea

Aral Sea

Sea of Japan

Pacific Ocean

Arabian Sea

Bay of Bengal

South China Sea

Indian Ocean

Key

☐ 0–1,000
▨ 1,000–5,000
■ 5,000 and above

Consumption per capita in kilograms of coal or its equivalent (1,000 kilograms = 450 pounds)

Energy Consumption

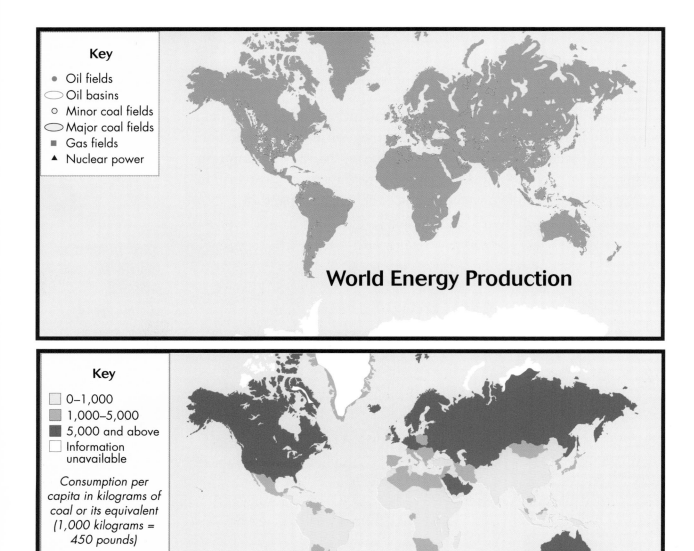

Key

- Oil fields
- Oil basins
- Minor coal fields
- Major coal fields
- Gas fields
- Nuclear power

World Energy Production

Key

- 0–1,000
- 1,000–5,000
- 5,000 and above
- Information unavailable

Consumption per capita in kilograms of coal or its equivalent (1,000 kilograms = 450 pounds)

World Energy Consumption

▲ *Above: The most industrialized nations of the world—including Japan—are the major producers of nuclear energy. They also consume a lot of energy.*

Finally, take a look at the map of worldwide harmful emissions of fossil fuels on the opposite page. Here you can see how Asia is affected by the burning of coal and oil, and compare it to other areas of the world. Harmful emissions from the burning of fossil fuels contribute to environmental problems such as global warming, destruction of the ozone layer, and acid rain.

The Environment

A look at the environmental damage map on page 30 shows that Asia's environmental problems are concentrated in the southern and western regions of the continent.

Acid rain is a significant problem. The gases in the atmosphere that produce it come mainly from burning coal, oil, gas, and wood in order to operate vehicles and to produce heat and cooking fuel for homes and workplaces. Acid rain weakens and destroys trees and plants and pollutes water, killing any fish that live there. Eastern China has already been affected by acid rain created by factories and the burning of wood for fuel. In Southeast Asia, the destruction of tropical forests is contributing to acid rain as well as to dangerously high levels of air pollution. The forests of Indonesia are burned to clear land for large-scale plantation farming. In India, too, forests are burned to increase agricultural space.

Asia's coastal pollution is caused by several factors: factory waste, shipping, and severe overcrowding, especially in the major cities of Japan, China, and India.

Compare the land use map and the environmental damage map. You can see that the areas of human-induced desertification are in

▼ *Below: Russia and the United States produce more fossil fuel emissions than other nations.*

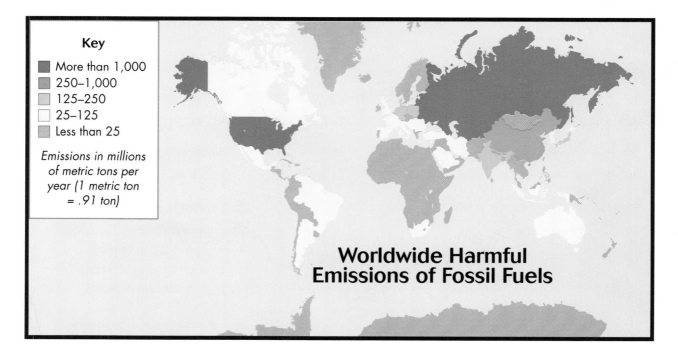

Key

■ More than 1,000
■ 250–1,000
□ 125–250
□ 25–125
■ Less than 25

Emissions in millions of metric tons per year (1 metric ton = .91 ton)

Worldwide Harmful Emissions of Fossil Fuels

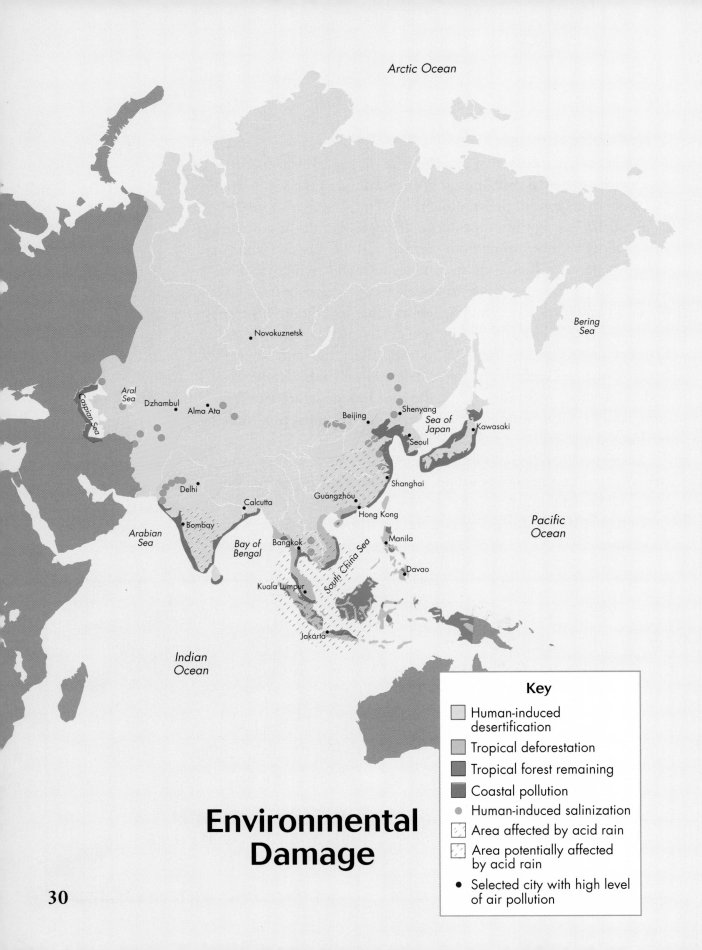

Environmental Damage

Key

- Human-induced desertification
- Tropical deforestation
- Tropical forest remaining
- Coastal pollution
- Human-induced salinization
- Area affected by acid rain
- Area potentially affected by acid rain
- Selected city with high level of air pollution

several cotton-growing regions. Intensive farming methods used in these areas, including the increased use of chemicals, have worn out the soil. In addition, over-irrigation is damaging the land. This is shown by the points of human-induced salinization. In these areas, intensive irrigation is washing the nutrients from the soil, leaving it encrusted with salts. This salinized land is unsuitable for raising crops or grazing livestock.

Increased irrigation has also reduced the size of the Aral Sea. Water for some irrigation projects—such as the Kara Kum Canal in Turkmenistan—is drawn from rivers that feed into the Aral Sea. The effect on this saltwater lake has been dramatic. In 1960, the Aral Sea was more than 175 feet (53 meters) deep and covered 25,800 square miles (66,822 square kilometers) of land. In 1987, its depth had been reduced to 43 feet, and aerial mapping showed that its area had decreased by 40 percent. This means that a portion of the lake the size of Belgium had disappeared. Now, the leftover salt, sand, and dust are blowing into agricultural areas and killing the crops. In addition, the climate around the lake is becoming harsher and less suitable for agriculture. Some geographers think that the Aral Sea may be gone by the year 2020.

◀◀ *Opposite:* Asia's crowded coastal cities pollute the waters along the shoreline.

A Closer Look

You can learn a lot about what a place is like by looking at different kinds of maps one at a time. However, by comparing the information presented in two or more maps, you can discover something about how and why it got that way.

Compare the environmental damage and population density maps of Asia (pages 30 and 48). How does the population map help explain the location of environmental problems?

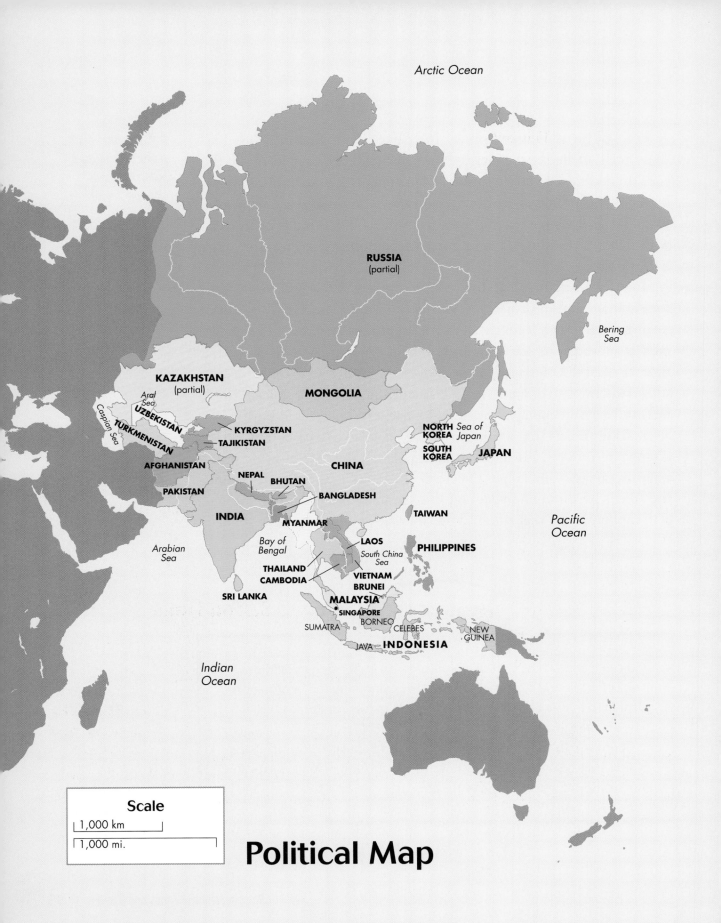

Arctic Ocean

RUSSIA
(partial)

Bering
Sea

KAZAKHSTAN
(partial)

Aral
Sea

MONGOLIA

UZBEKISTAN

Caspian Sea

TURKMENISTAN

KYRGYZSTAN

TAJIKISTAN

NORTH
KOREA

Sea of
Japan

SOUTH
KOREA

JAPAN

AFGHANISTAN

CHINA

NEPAL

BHUTAN

PAKISTAN

BANGLADESH

TAIWAN

INDIA

MYANMAR

Pacific
Ocean

Arabian
Sea

Bay of
Bengal

LAOS

PHILIPPINES

South China
Sea

THAILAND

CAMBODIA

VIETNAM

BRUNEI

SRI LANKA

MALAYSIA

SINGAPORE

SUMATRA

BORNEO

CELEBES

NEW
GUINEA

JAVA

INDONESIA

Indian
Ocean

Scale

1,000 km

1,000 mi.

Political Map

Chapter **2**

Mapping People, Cultures, and the Political World

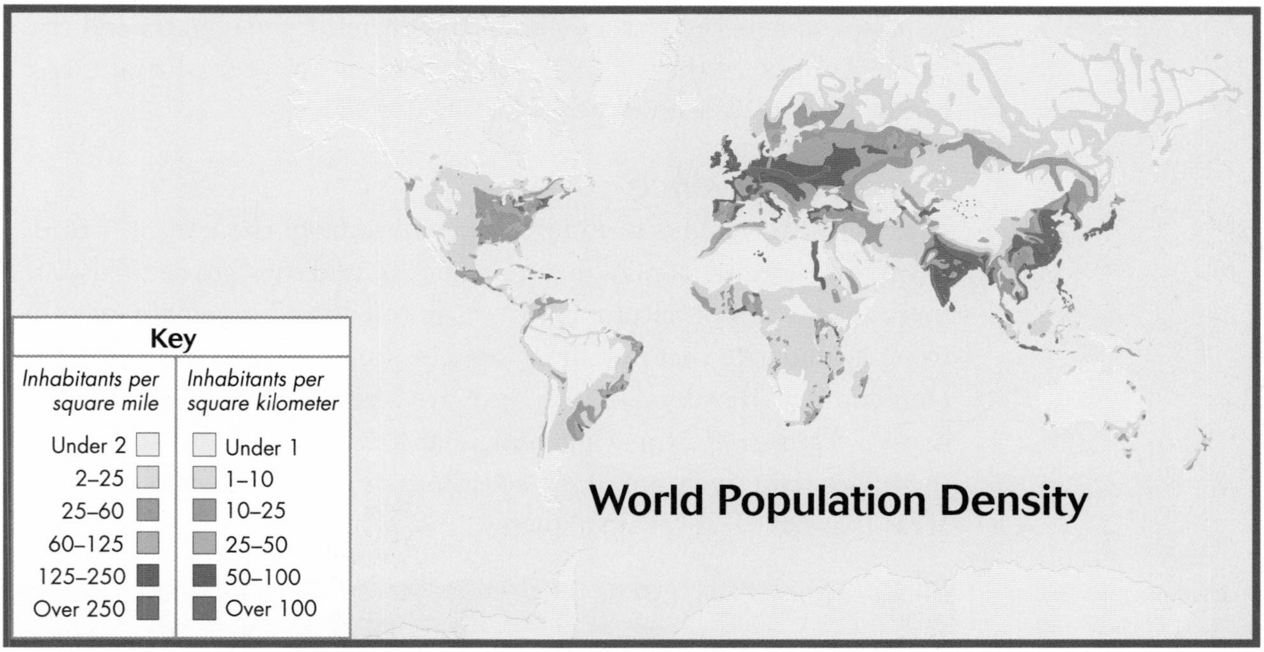

Key

Inhabitants per square mile	Inhabitants per square kilometer
Under 2	Under 1
2–25	1–10
25–60	10–25
60–125	25–50
125–250	50–100
Over 250	Over 100

World Population Density

Maps can reveal much more about a place than simply what it is like physically. They can also tell you a great deal about the political divisions of the area. Maps can inform you about the cultures and customs of the people who live there as well. They can show you the languages spoken in a region, the religions people identify with, and the places where most people live.

▲ *Above: India is one of the most densely populated countries in the world.*

◀◀ *Opposite: Many Asian nations did not gain their independence until after World War II.*

33

The Political World: Dividing the Land

Political maps such as the one on page 32 are familiar to everyone. In these, there is no attempt to show what an area physically looks like. Rather, a political map shows the boundaries that separate countries (or states and provinces). Colors are used to distinguish one country from another. A political map may also show capitals and major cities, as the map on the opposite page does.

Boundaries are artificial; that is, they are created, set, and changed by people. Conquests, wars, and treaties have all caused boundary changes. Political maps can, therefore, also be a guide to the history of a region.

Geographers keep track of boundary changes, and country and city name changes, as they occur, so that new, up-to-date political maps can be created as soon as possible.

Nature's Influence

The political world is not entirely separate from the natural world. Rivers or mountains may dictate where boundaries are set. Also, if there is a wealth of natural resources in one location, people may try to set boundaries that put all or most of those resources within their own country's borders. Cities, too, are often located according to natural features. Comparing climate and major city maps will show that cities tend to cluster along coastlines or major waterways, and in areas that have less severe climates.

▶ *Right:* Hong Kong, located on the South China Sea, is a major commercial center.

▶▶ *Opposite:* Southern Asia's coastline is dotted with capitals and major cities.

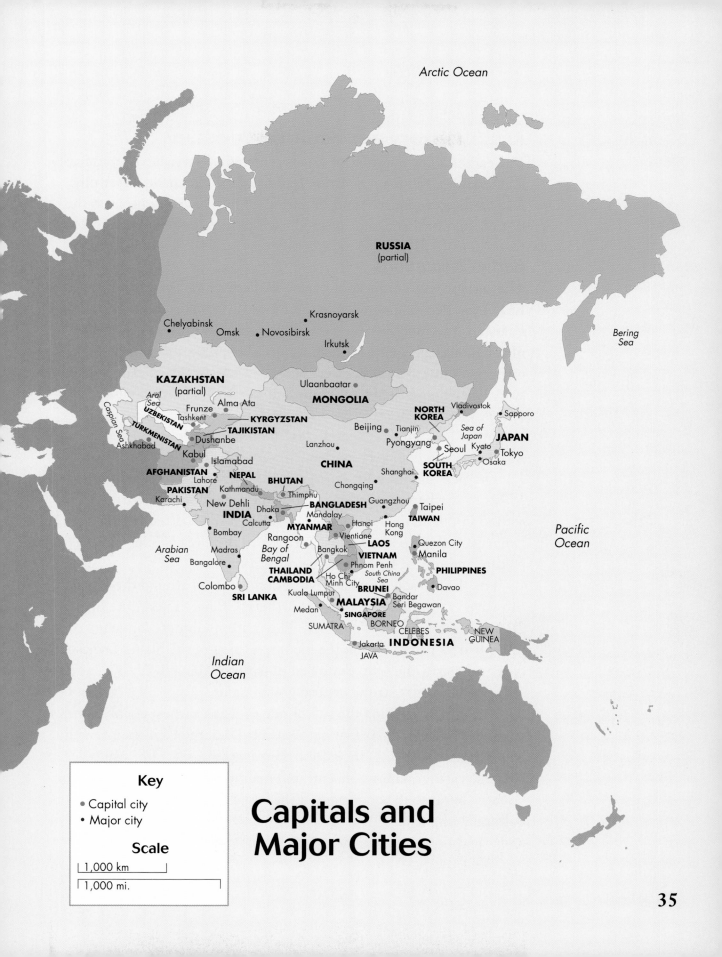

Arctic Ocean

RUSSIA
(partial)

Bering
Sea

Chelyabinsk
Omsk
Novosibirsk
Krasnoyarsk
Irkutsk

KAZAKHSTAN
(partial)

Aral
Sea
Frunze
Alma Ata
Ulaanbaatar
MONGOLIA

UZBEKISTAN
Tashkent
KYRGYZSTAN
NORTH
KOREA
Vladivostok
Sapporo

Caspian Sea
TAJIKISTAN
Beijing
Tianjin
Sea of
Japan
JAPAN

TURKMENISTAN
Dushanbe
Lanzhou
Pyongyang
Seoul
Kyoto
Tokyo

Ashkhabad
Kabul
Osaka

Islamabad
CHINA
Shanghai
SOUTH
KOREA

AFGHANISTAN
NEPAL
Chongqing

PAKISTAN
Lahore
Kathmandu
BHUTAN
Guangzhou

Karachi
New Dehli
Thimphu
BANGLADESH
Taipei

Dhaka
Hong
Kong
TAIWAN

INDIA
Calcutta
Mandalay
Hanoi

Bombay
MYANMAR
Vientiane

Rangoon
LAOS
Quezon City

Arabian
Sea
Madras
Bangkok
VIETNAM
Manila

Bangalore
Bay of
Bengal
THAILAND
Phnom Penh
South China
Sea
PHILIPPINES

Colombo
CAMBODIA
Ho Chi
Minh City
Davao

SRI LANKA
Kuala Lumpur
BRUNEI

Medan
MALAYSIA
Bandar
Seri Begawan

SINGAPORE

SUMATRA
BORNEO
CELEBES
NEW
GUINEA

Jakarta
INDONESIA

JAVA

Pacific
Ocean

Indian
Ocean

Key

• Capital city
• Major city

Scale

1,000 km

1,000 mi.

Capitals and Major Cities

Asia's History and Political Divisions

The earliest known history of Asia is centered on its river valleys, areas that today are still the population centers of the continent. Over time, Asia has been conquered and colonized; it has shut itself off from the rest of the world and later opened itself to international trade.

Early Civilizations

The earliest Asian civilizations arose in the river valleys of South and East Asia. People have lived in the Indus River valley of what is now Pakistan since about 2500 B.C. Archaeological excavations of one major Indus valley city, Mohenjo-daro, show that it was surprisingly modern. The city's streets were laid out in a regular pattern. Multi-story brick houses had bathrooms and were connected to city-wide sewer systems. An intricate series of dams and canals provided irrigation for crops. It seems clear that the people who lived in Mohenjo-daro enjoyed a settled, agricultural lifestyle.

The next great South Asian civilization was established in the 1500s B.C., when the Aryans, a nomadic people from Central Asia, settled in northern India. They developed the written Sanskrit language and introduced ideas that formed the basis of later Indian culture and practices, such as the caste system.

The third cradle of Asian civilization centered around the Huang Ho River valley in what is now northern China. There, the Shang Dynasty arose in the 1700s B.C. The written Chinese language of today had its beginnings in the picture-writing of the Shang Dynasty. A later dynasty, the Qin, united all of eastern China in 221 B.C. and set up China's first strong central government.

Not only was China the site of one of Asia's earliest civilizations, it was the home of Asia's first mapmakers. Until the Chinese invented paper around 100 B.C., they drew their maps on silk. For centuries, Chinese cartographers concentrated mainly on mapping their own country because they considered the rest of the world to be less culturally important.

Invasions

Huns from Central Asia conquered northern China in the A.D. 300s and by the 500s had overthrown India's Gupta Empire as well. In 1206, another invasion came from Central Asia. At that time, the warrior Genghis Khan united the various Mongol tribes living in Mongolia and set out on a career of conquest. At its height, the Mongol Empire stretched from the Pacific Ocean west to the Danube River in Europe. Only northernmost Asia, and South and Southeast Asia were not under Mongol rule.

During the reign of Genghis's grandson Khublai Khan, 17-year-old Marco Polo traveled from his home in Venice to Khublai Khan's court in China. Polo, along with his father and uncle, did diplomatic work for Khublai Khan for 17 years, traveling throughout Asia. Although Polo did not map his journeys, tales of his travels and the riches he had seen were published in a book after he returned home.

▼ **Below:** *Genghis Khan united the Mongols and became the ruler of the Mongol Empire from 1206 until 1227, when he died.*

▲ **Above:** *Marco Polo wrote his famous account of his travels in 1298.*

These stories inspired European cartographers to draw maps based on Polo's descriptions of Asia, and excited traders, who began searching for a sea route to the Far East.

The Mongol Empire fell in 1368 without ever affecting South Asia. However, in 1526, a descendant of Genghis Khan invaded India and established the Mogul Empire, which covered almost all of what is now South Asia.

The next series of invasions would come from the West—the invasions of European merchants expanding their trading empires.

Western Conquests

During the 1500s and 1600s, various European countries staked their claims in Asia. They wanted to secure trading rights to the continent's spices, silks, furs, and minerals.

Portugal took control of ports in China, Japan, Malaysia, and Ceylon (now called Sri Lanka). The Philippines was taken over by Spain, and what is now Indonesia was occupied by The Netherlands and became known as the Dutch East Indies. The British East India Company—a powerful British trading company—established bases in India and gradually took control of most of India as well as Sri Lanka and Burma (now Myanmar). European Russians moved into North Asia looking to establish trade in furs and minerals.

During the early part of the 1600s, Japan and China took back control of their trading ports and stopped almost all trade with Europe.

As European merchants and missionaries established a permanent presence in Asia, their knowledge of the continent led to ever more accurate maps. Sometimes this information went both ways. For example, in the late 1500s, Italian missionary Matteo Ricci combined his own knowledge of China with existing Chinese maps to make new maps to send to Europe. He also introduced the Chinese to maps based on European discoveries and exploration. In this way he expanded Chinese knowledge of the "barbarian" world beyond the borders of China, which they considered the center of the civilized world.

Colonialism

By the late 1700s, most of India was under British control, either directly or indirectly, as the map below shows. The territory was governed by the British East India Company. The British expanded their territory by acquiring additional Indian-ruled states (colored blue on the map). They then further increased their hold over Indian lands by offering subsidiary alliances to Indian rulers. This means that the East India Company would provide troops to help protect an Indian state from outside attack, in return for which the state would pay the company money and allow it to control the state's relations with other countries. The Marathas were an independent Indian group that controlled much of western and central India (colored green on the map). By the mid-1800s, the British had overthrown the last of the Indian rulers and expanded their colonial empire over not only India, but also the adjoining territory and Malaysia.

India Under British Control

Key
- British Territory, 1797
- British acquisitions, 1797–1805
- States under subsidiary alliances
- Maratha lands, 1805

◀ **Left:** *By 1805, the British controlled all of India except for the land occupied by the Marathas.*

39

The Russian Empire controlled North Asia and much of western Asia. The Netherlands continued to hold Indonesia, and the French took control over the easternmost part of the southeast Asian peninsula. This area, known as French Indochina, made up what is now Vietnam, Laos, and Cambodia.

China and Japan continued to be independent, although certain Chinese ports, such as Hong Kong, were under European colonial rule.

The Chinese Struggle

From the 1920s to the 1940s, China struggled to maintain a unified country. As you can see from the map below, there was conflict between the Chinese Nationalist party, or Kuomintang, and the Communist party. The Northern Campaign of the Nationalists in

▼ **Below:** China was a very unsettled region in the 1920s, '30s, and '40s.

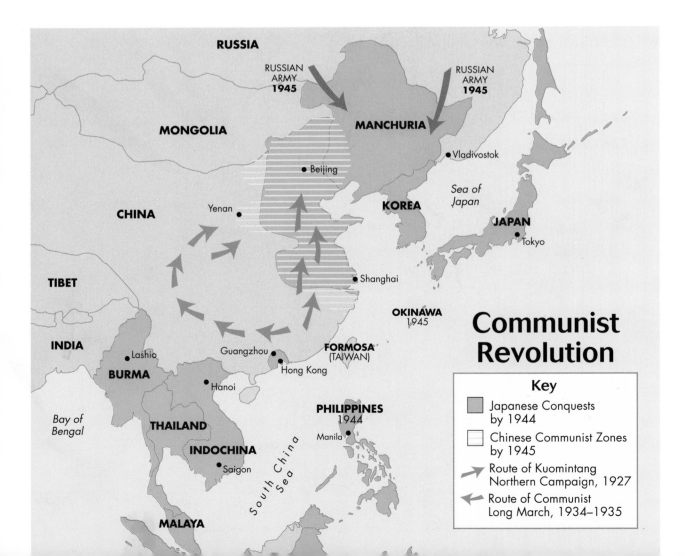

Communist Revolution

Key

- Japanese Conquests by 1944
- Chinese Communist Zones by 1945
- → Route of Kuomintang Northern Campaign, 1927
- ← Route of Communist Long March, 1934–1935

1927 (shown in green arrows on the map) resulted in the establishment of Nationalist China. A few years later, Nationalist forces drove the Communists out of southern China. The Communists' "Long March" to the north to a new base in Yenan is indicated by the purple arrows on the map. During World War II, the Chinese suffered more military struggles when the Japanese and Russians invaded. On October 1, 1949, the People's Republic of China was proclaimed by the Communists after a three-year civil war.

Independence

Only a few Asian countries were independent before World War I: the Union of Soviet Socialist Republic (now Russia and the republics of Kazakhstan, Kyrgyzstan, Tajikistan, Turkmenistan, and Uzbekistan), Afghanistan, Nepal, China, Japan, Macao (as a Portuguese protectorate), and Thailand. Most of the rest of Asia gained its independence after World War II ended in 1945.

Since that time, the map face of Asia has continued to change as a result of religious and political conflicts, and will probably do so for some time to come. For example, British-controlled India was divided along religious lines in 1947. Muslim areas were designated as East and West Pakistan. India itself was predominantly Hindu. There were many struggles between the Pakistani units until East Pakistan became the independent state of Bangladesh in 1971. Religious conflict between Muslims and Hindus in Kashmir—an area divided between Pakistan and northern India—shows no sign of resolution.

The most recent change in political boundaries took place in 1997, when Hong Kong became part of China. It was previously under British rule.

Population, Language, and Religion

Political maps tell us about the boundaries of a nation, but not about the lives of its inhabitants. Maps that focus on population, language, and religion tell us more about a country's people. Most countries'

Key

- Decrease
- 0–1%
- 1–2%
- 2–3%
- >3%

(Does not include effects of migration)

**World Annual Average
Population Growth**

▲ *Above: The populations of North Asia, Australia, and the United States are growing much more slowly than the populations of other regions.*

▼ *Below: Asia represents more language groups than any other continent.*

governments conduct a census (population count) on some sort of regular basis. The United States, for example, has conducted a regular 10-year census since 1790.

Census figures are used to make maps that show how population is distributed. The world population density map on page 33 is one such map. By compiling statistics over a period of years—from census and birth and death records—geographers can make predictions regarding population growth, as shown in the map above.

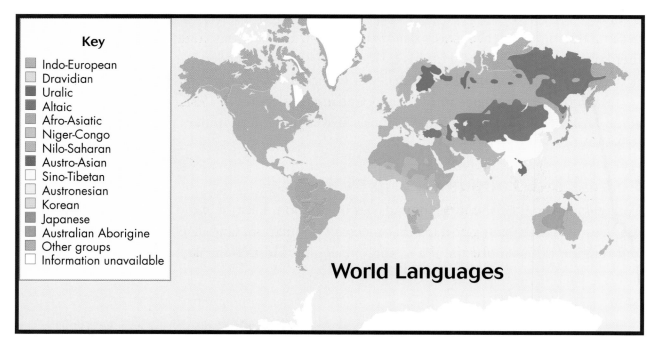

Key

- Indo-European
- Dravidian
- Uralic
- Altaic
- Afro-Asiatic
- Niger-Congo
- Nilo-Saharan
- Austro-Asian
- Sino-Tibetan
- Austronesian
- Korean
- Japanese
- Australian Aborigine
- Other groups
- Information unavailable

World Languages

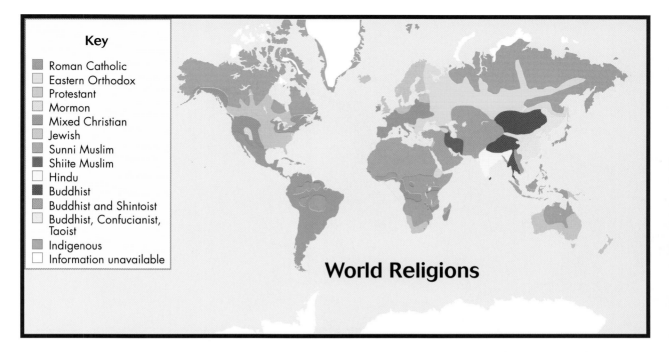

Key

- Roman Catholic
- Eastern Orthodox
- Protestant
- Mormon
- Mixed Christian
- Jewish
- Sunni Muslim
- Shiite Muslim
- Hindu
- Buddhist
- Buddhist and Shintoist
- Buddhist, Confucianist, Taoist
- Indigenous
- Information unavailable

World Religions

Because many different languages may be spoken in any one country, it is difficult to map language distribution precisely. However, large areas that represent language families can be mapped, as shown in the map on the opposite page. In the same way, predominant religions of an area can also be mapped, as shown in the world religions map above.

▲ *Above:* In Asia and Africa, Christian religions are in the minority.

Asian Religions

Most of the world's major religions are well represented in Asia. A look at the map on page 44 will show how they are distributed throughout the continent.

Hinduism is the main religion of India and Nepal, while Buddhism is the primary religion in large areas of Central and Southeast Asia. As you can see on the map, Buddhism, in combination with other religions, is also important in East Asia. Many Chinese practice Confucianism or Taoism, and many Japanese are Shintoists.

Reflecting its Spanish history, most of the Philippines is Roman Catholic. Its southern end is Sunni Muslim, as is the majority of Indonesia, Malaysia, Bangladesh, and most of the western portion of the continent outside Russia. In Russia, the majority of the people

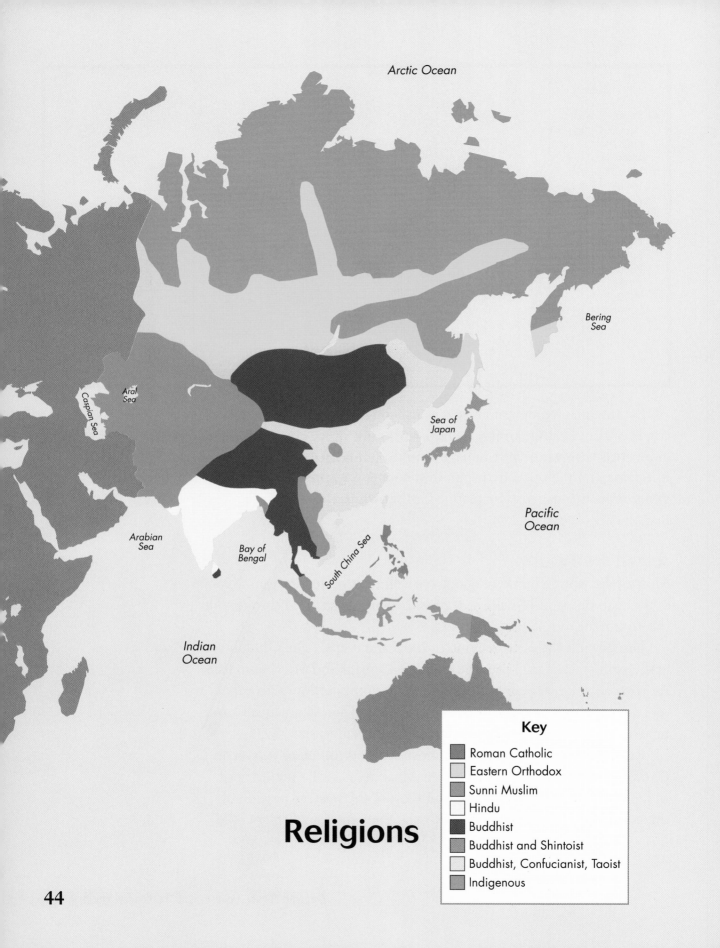

Arctic Ocean

Bering
Sea

Caspian Sea

Aral
Sea

Sea of
Japan

Pacific
Ocean

Arabian
Sea

Bay of
Bengal

South China Sea

Indian
Ocean

Key

- Roman Catholic
- Eastern Orthodox
- Sunni Muslim
- Hindu
- Buddhist
- Buddhist and Shintoist
- Buddhist, Confucianist, Taoist
- Indigenous

Religions

◀ **Left:** This golden buddha is in a temple in Thailand.

◀◀ **Opposite:** India and Nepal are the only Asian nations where Hinduism is the dominant religion.

are Eastern Orthodox. Indigenous religions are important primarily in parts of Southeast Asia and in the extreme north. Many of these religions are based on a belief in spirits.

Asian Languages

As you can see from the map on page 46, most of the major language families are represented in Asia. People in the East and Southeast speak Sino-Tibetan languages, colored light yellow on the map. Chinese is the most widespread of these languages.

Russian, and the languages of northern India, Pakistan, and Afghanistan belong to the Indo-European language family, colored light green. The Dravidian language family is represented by the languages spoken in southern India and northern Sri Lanka.

Throughout Central Asia and a large portion of North Asia the main language family is Altaic. Uralic is found in parts of northern Russia. Japanese and Korean are their own language families. The languages of the Austro-Asian family are spoken in Laos, Vietnam, and Cambodia. Indonesian and Malaysian languages belong to the Austronesian language family.

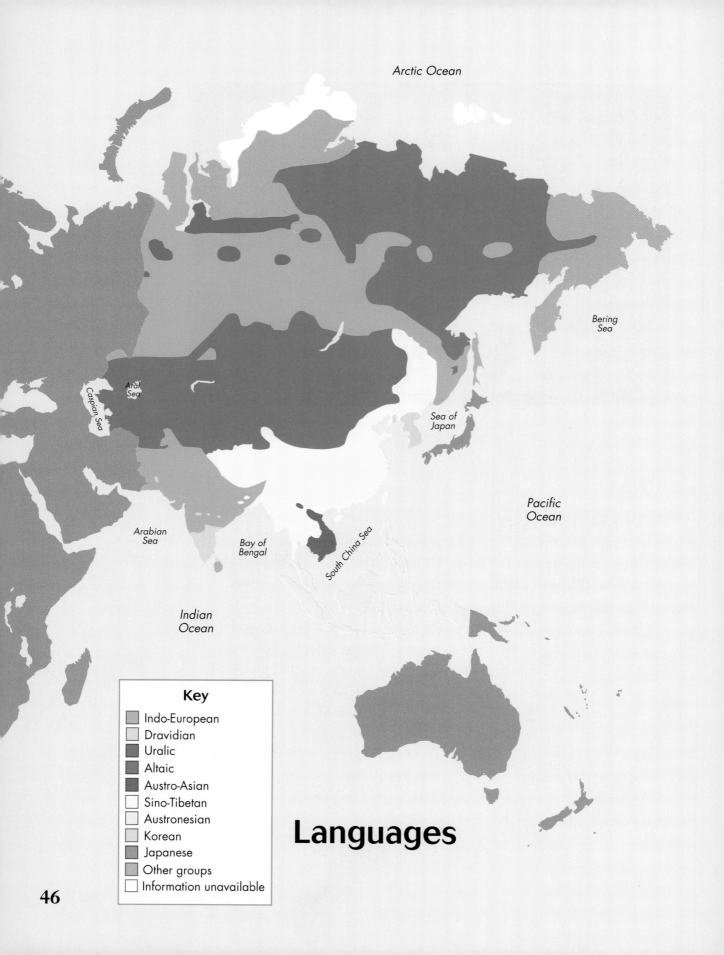

Arctic Ocean

Bering
Sea

Caspian Sea

Aral
Sea

Sea of
Japan

Pacific
Ocean

Arabian
Sea

Bay of
Bengal

South China Sea

Indian
Ocean

Key

- Indo-European
- Dravidian
- Uralic
- Altaic
- Austro-Asian
- Sino-Tibetan
- Austronesian
- Korean
- Japanese
- Other groups
- Information unavailable

Languages

Asian Population Growth and Density

There are more people living in Asia than on any other continent—about 3.5 billion people, or 60 percent of the world's population. Since Asia is also the largest continent, this huge population would pose no problems if it were evenly distributed. However, as you can see by the population density map on page 48, this is not the case.

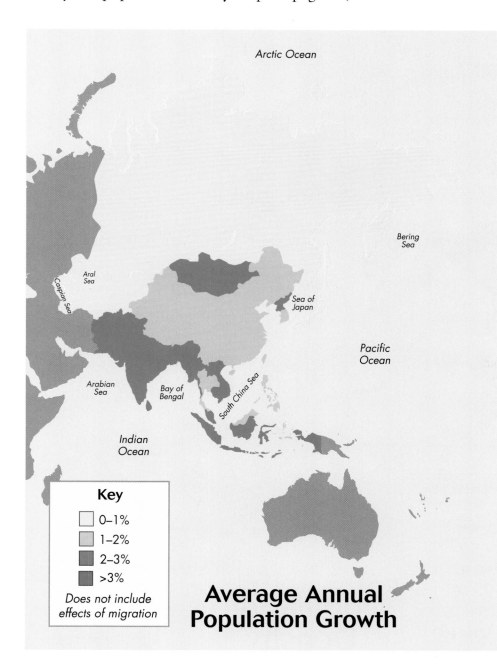

Arctic Ocean

Aral Sea

Caspian Sea

Bering Sea

Sea of Japan

Pacific Ocean

Arabian Sea

Bay of Bengal

South China Sea

Indian Ocean

Key

- 0–1%
- 1–2%
- 2–3%
- >3%

Does not include effects of migration

Average Annual Population Growth

◀ *Left:* China's population growth has slowed down because the government encourages couples to have only one child.

◀◀ *Opposite:* The people of Russia, Pakistan, Afghanistan, and northern India all speak languages from the Indo-European family.

47

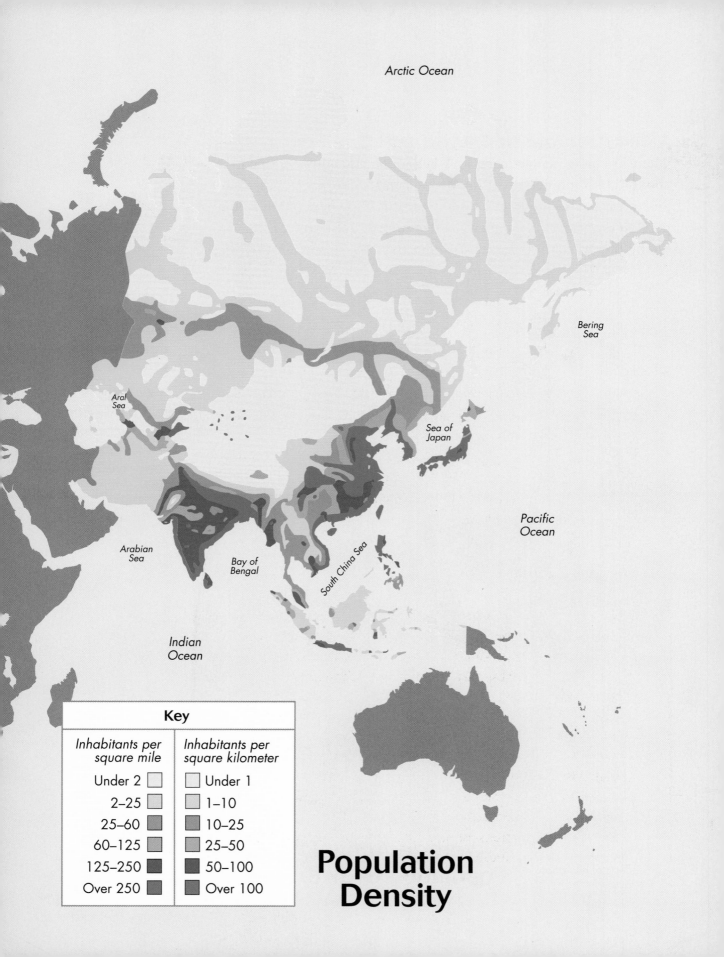

Arctic Ocean

Bering
Sea

Aral
Sea

Sea of
Japan

Pacific
Ocean

Arabian
Sea

Bay of
Bengal

South China Sea

Indian
Ocean

Key	
Inhabitants per square mile	Inhabitants per square kilometer
Under 2	Under 1
2–25	1–10
25–60	10–25
60–125	25–50
125–250	50–100
Over 250	Over 100

Population Density

The majority of Asia's people are crowded into a relatively small area in South and East Asia. In fact, China is the world's most populated country, and India is the second most populated country. Together they contain more than a third of the world's people. As you can see from the map on page 47, however, China's rate of population growth is less than India's. If the two countries maintain their current growth rates, India will rank first in world population in less than 50 years.

◀◀ *Opposite:* While China's population is thinner in the west, India's population is dense throughout the country.

Per Capita GDP

Gross Domestic Product (GDP) is the total output of a country—all products and labor. Dividing the value of a country's GDP by its population gives the per capita (per person) GDP. This figure represents the average annual income of that country's people. Generally speaking, more industrialized countries have a higher GDP—and a better economy—than less industrialized countries.

In Asia, for example, Japan—one of the world's leading industrial nations—had a per capita GDP of $16,950 in 1990. In contrast, Bangladesh, which relies on a traditional agricultural economy, had a 1990 per capita GDP of $1,050.

A Closer Look

People choose the places they live for many different reasons. One person may decide on a rural area where there is land suitable for farming. Another might settle along a transportation route, or where there is a pleasant climate.

Look at the population density map on the opposite page. Notice the settlement pattern in North Asia. The map on page 35 doesn't show any major cities in that region, and the land use map on page 21 shows that the land wouldn't be attractive to farmers. What do you think might help account for the location of small population groups (marked in yellow)? Compare the population density map with the physical, climate, and transportation routes maps on pages 10, 16, and 50 to answer the question.

Transportation Routes

Arctic Ocean

Bering Sea

Pacific Ocean

Sovetskaya Gavan
Khabarovsk
Omsk
Novosibirsk
Irkutsk
Ulaanbaatar
Vladivostok
Sea of Japan
Tokyo
Osaka
Seoul
Pusan
Pyongyang
Beijing
Tashkent
Aral Sea
Caspian Sea
Kabul
Islamabad
Xi'an
Kagoshima
Wuhan
Shanghai
Chongqing
New Dehli
Kathmandu
Thimphu
Guangzhou
Taipei
Karachi
Dhaka
Hong Kong
Calcutta
Hanoi
Bombay
Rangoon
Bay of Bengal
Bangkok
Phnom Penh
South China Sea
Manila
Madras
Arabian Sea
Colombo
Kuala Lumpur
Singapore
Bander Seri Begawan
Indian Ocean
Jakarta

Key

— Major roadway
— Navigational route
— Railroad
△ Major port
✈ Major airport

Scale

1,000 km

1,000 mi.

Chapter 3

Mapping the World Through Which We Move

In addition to showing us the physical and political characteristics of the world, maps can also have a more practical, "hands on" purpose: They can assist us in moving through our world. Whether that world is an entire continent, a single city, or the second floor of an art museum, different maps provide us with the information we need to get from one point to another.

Maps Show the Way

Whenever we want to get from one place to another, maps can help us plan our routes by showing the options that are available. Maps show where roads are located and what kind of roads they are. They can also tell us whether we can take an airplane, train, bus, or other form of transportation to get there. Once we reach our destination, maps again can help us plan how best to get around—on foot, by car, or by some kind of public transportation.

Creating Road and City Maps

To create road maps and city maps, mapmakers (cartographers) look first for base data maps that accurately position points to be included

◄◄ *Opposite:* Asia's major seaports are in the south, where the harbor waters do not freeze.

on the new map. These base maps might be acquired from the federal government, states, or cities. Aerial photographs may be taken to show if, and how, any areas may have changed since the base map was made.

Then, cartographers contact agencies that can provide specific information about street names—names that will be the most help to a person traveling in the area. Other agencies are contacted to determine which buildings or other points of interest are important and should be included on the map of the area. Field work—actually visiting the area being mapped—adds useful first-hand information.

Scale also plays an important part in determining what is shown on a map. The smaller the scale, the more carefully cartographers must pick and choose the details that are being included. Careful selection is needed in order to keep a map from becoming too cluttered.

The transportation and city maps in this chapter provide still more ways to look at and learn about the continent, countries, and cities.

Transportation in Asia

A look at the map on page 50 shows that the highest concentration of major transportation routes on the continent are in South Asia and mainland Southeast Asia. Aside from rivers and lakes, only limited transportation routes exist in Central Asia, and none at all in most of North Asia. To understand why, compare the transportation map with the population density map on page 48.

Roads

Few rural roads in Asia are paved, and vast areas of the continent—particularly North Asia—have no roads at all. Major roadways connect capital cities with each other, and they connect industrial centers with port cities. During the monsoon season in South and Southeast Asia, many roads become impassable because of flooding.

Most Asians do not own cars, and those who do live in the cities. Even in the cities, however, the vast majority use public transportation or walk to reach their destinations.

Railroads

Railroads provide a major means of long-distance transportation throughout Asia, both for goods and people. As you can see from the transportation routes map, traveling by rail is the only way to cross Russia. The Trans-Siberian Railroad, which runs from Moscow in European Russia to Vladivostok on the Pacific Ocean, is the world's longest railway at 5,600 miles (9,012 kilometers).

As you can see by comparing the transportation map on page 50 with the major cities map on page 35, railroads connect most of the important cities in Asia. They also offer transport between inland resources and coastal and port cities. Many of the lines running inland from the coast were established by the colonial rulers during the 1800s. They set up the lines to bring raw materials to ports for export back to Europe.

Waterways

Rivers have long provided a means of transportation in Asia for both people and goods, especially in the south. Residents of rural areas are especially dependent on rivers, since other forms of transportation are scarce. For these people, owning a boat is essential. Many large Asian cities are located on water, and in these cities, boats often serve as houses in addition to providing transportation.

The major river systems in North Asia are not used very often for transportation. Siberian rivers are frozen for about nine months out of the year. The ports in that region also stay frozen for much of the year, which explains why Asia's important seaports are in the south.

Airlines

Airlines provide one of the easiest ways of moving people across the huge distances and rugged terrain of Asia. They connect most large cities within the continent. The major airports marked on the map offer overseas flights as well. Three cities—Tokyo, Seoul, and Hong Kong—have airports that rank among the world's busiest.

Other Transportation

Walking is a primary mode of transportation throughout Asia. Bicycles are popular in cities, and tricycle-like pedicabs supplement taxicabs in China. In Thailand you'll find small, motorized three-wheeled taxis. Subway systems operate in many of Asia's major cities, such as Tokyo, Hong Kong, and Calcutta. Ferries provide transportation between some cities in island nations such as Indonesia. In rural Asia, animals such as oxen, yaks, water buffalo, and elephants are used to carry freight or pull wagons.

▲ *Above: Many residents of Beijing get around the city on bicycles.*

The Cities of Asia

As you refer to the maps in this section, notice that railroads figure prominently on every one. This reflects the importance of rail transportation in Asia.

Tokyo

The world's most populous city is Tokyo, the capital of Japan. The city was named Edo when it was established in 1457, and renamed Tokyo in 1868. The Imperial Palace, at the center of the map on the opposite page, is the residence of Japan's emperor. To the east of the palace is Uchibori-dori Avenue, which means "Inner Moat Avenue," a reference to the fact that moats separate the palace and its grounds from the rest of the city. A bit farther east you'll find Tokyo's main train station.

To the west, in the Meiji Jingu Outer Gardens, is the National Stadium. Built for the 1964 Summer Olympics, it is the largest stadium in Japan.

Tokyo's many parks and gardens offer a restful change of scene from the crowded and noisy city streets. Popular Ueno Park, set on a hill northeast of the Imperial Palace, is one of Japan's first public parks. Here you'll find a number of museums, a music hall, and the city zoo.

Look at the northern end of the island in the southeast corner of the Tokyo map. Sumiyoshi Myojin Shrine was established by fisherman from Osaka when they first settled here. It houses a statue of the god who protects fishermen. Southwest across the river, you'll find the Central Wholesale Market—Asia's largest fish market. The Bridgestone Museum of Art, to the north, houses one of the best private collections of art in Japan. The nearby Kite Museum celebrates kites and kite flying, a popular pastime in Japan. The National Museum of Modern Art, north of the Imperial Palace, features the works of Japanese artists. Continuing counterclockwise around the Inner Loop Expressway, you come to the National Theater and the Supreme Court.

▼ **Below:** *The Imperial Palace and the National Museum of Art are separated from the rest of the city by moats, or water-filled ditches.*

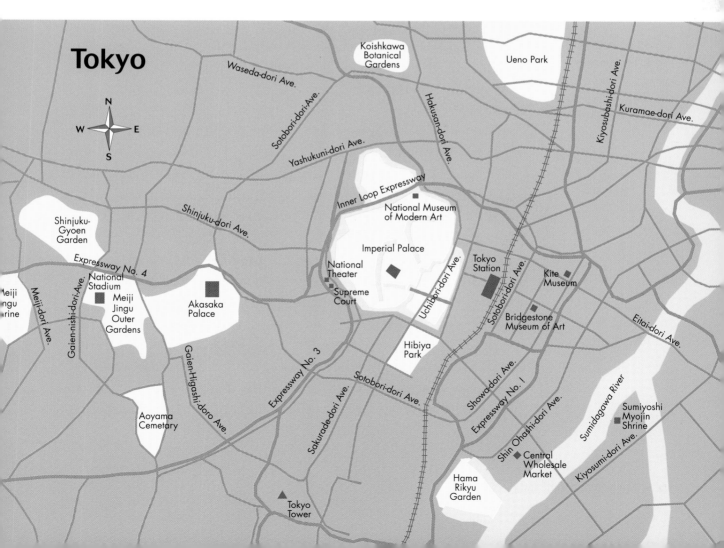

Tokyo

Koishkawa Botanical Gardens

Ueno Park

Waseda-dori Ave.

Sotobori-dori Ave.

Hakusan-dori Ave.

Kiyosubashi-dori Ave.

Kuramae-dori Ave.

Yashukuni-dori Ave.

Shinjuku-dori Ave.

Inner Loop Expressway

National Museum of Modern Art

Shinjuku-Gyoen Garden

Imperial Palace

Expressway No. 4

Tokyo Station

Uchibori-dori Ave.

Sotobori-dori Ave.

Kite Museum

Meiji Jingu Shrine

Gaien-nishi-dori Ave.

National Stadium

Meiji Jingu Outer Gardens

Akasaka Palace

National Theater

Supreme Court

Bridgestone Museum of Art

Eitai-dori Ave.

Meiji-dori Ave.

Hibiya Park

Gaien-Higashi-doro Ave.

Expressway No. 3

Sakurade-dori Ave.

Sotobori-dori Ave.

Showa-dori Ave.

Expressway No. 1

Shin Ohashi-dori Ave.

Sumidagawa River

Sumiyoshi Myojin Shrine

Aoyama Cemetary

Central Wholesale Market

Kiyosumi-dori Ave.

Tokyo Tower

Hama Rikyu Garden

Both of these buildings were designed by the winners of a design competition held when Tokyo was being rebuilt after the devastation of World War II.

Bombay

Bombay is India's largest city and a major west coast port. It is an island city, with an Indian and British history that is reflected in its varied landmarks. The older area of Bombay is on the southern end of the island—the area shown on the map on the opposite page. Here you'll find the city's historical and cultural landmarks, as well as its business center.

An important landmark is the Gateway of India, an 85-foot (26-meter) stone arch on the city's southeast coast. It was built to honor a state visit by Great Britain's King George V in 1911, while the city was still under British rule.

North of the Gateway, the Prince of Wales Museum, with its art, archaeology, and natural history exhibits, is a major attraction. An easy-to-spot landmark northwest of the museum is the 260-foot (79-meter) Rajabai clock tower, which is part of Bombay University.

Bombay's Indian and British history is reflected in the mix of Christian churches and Hindu temples scattered throughout the city. The oldest temple is Mahalaxmi Temple, in the northwest, built to honor the goddess of wealth. The Mumbadevi Temple, in the center of the city, is dedicated to Mumbai, goddess of the earth.

The large black rectangle in the western part of the city marks the location of two particularly interesting landmarks: the Hanging Gardens and the Towers of Silence. The beautiful "hanging" gardens are actually terraced gardens filled with topiary. These are plants that are

▼ *Below:* *Victoria Terminus, a railway station at the southern end of the map, is one of the largest buildings in Bombay.*

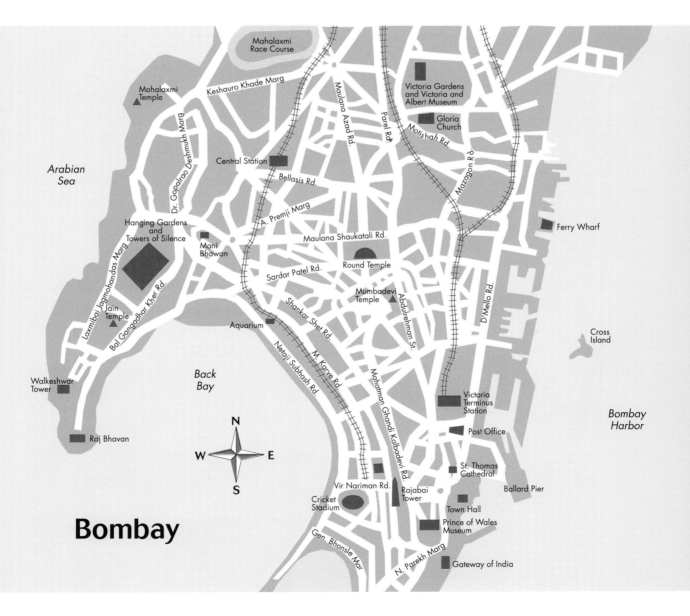

Mahalaxmi Race Course

Keshauro Khade Marg

Mahalaxmi Temple

Maulana Azad Rd.

Parel Rd.

Victoria Gardens and Victoria and Albert Museum

Gloria Church

Motishah Rd.

Dr. Gopalrao Deshmukh Marg

Central Station

Bellasis Rd.

Arabian Sea

Mazagon Rd.

Ferry Wharf

A. Premji Marg

Hanging Gardens and Towers of Silence

Mani Bhawan

Maulana Shaukatali Rd.

Round Temple

Sardar Patel Rd.

Mumbadevi Temple

Abdulrehman St.

Laxmibai Jagmohandas Marg

Jain Temple

Bal. Gangadhar Kher Rd.

Aquarium

Shankar Shet Rd.

D'Mello Rd.

Cross Island

Netaji Subhash Rd.

M. Karve Rd.

Back Bay

Mahatman Ghandi Kalbadevi Rd.

Walkeshwar Tower

Victoria Terminus Station

Bombay Harbor

Raj Bhavan

N

W   E

S

Post Office

St. Thomas Cathedral

Ballard Pier

Vir Nariman Rd.

Rajabai Tower

Town Hall

Bombay

Cricket Stadium

Prince of Wales Museum

Gen. Bhonsle Mar

N. Parekh Marg

Gateway of India

trained and pruned into a variety of designs or shapes, such as animals. The Towers of Silence are important to the Parsis, followers of the ancient Persian religion called Zoroastrianism. The Parsis lay their dead on top of the towers, which are surrounded by high walls. The remains are eaten by vultures.

The railroads and terminals that serve Bombay demonstrate the importance of rail transportation in India. The two largest terminals are Central Station, in the northwest, and Victoria Terminus, in the southeast. Victoria Terminus, with a life-size statue of Queen Victoria on top, is one of the largest buildings in Bombay. The first train out of Bombay left from this station in 1853.

Beijing

The map of Beijing on the opposite page shows the city's municipal district, which covers 6,873 square miles (17,801 square kilometers)—an area about the size of New Jersey. The district includes the central city, located northeast of the Botanical Gardens, as well as surrounding suburbs and farmland. This map was drawn on a much smaller scale than any of the previous city maps, allowing the mapmaker to show one of the most important landmarks of Beijing: the remnants of the Great Wall of China in the northern part of the district. The wall, built by hand over hundreds of years beginning in the early 200s B.C., was a 1,550-mile (2,494-kilometer) long fortification against northern invaders. Today it extends from the coast of China westward to the town of Jiayuguan.

▶ *Right:* The rooftops of Beijing are a mix of traditional and modern designs.

Beijing

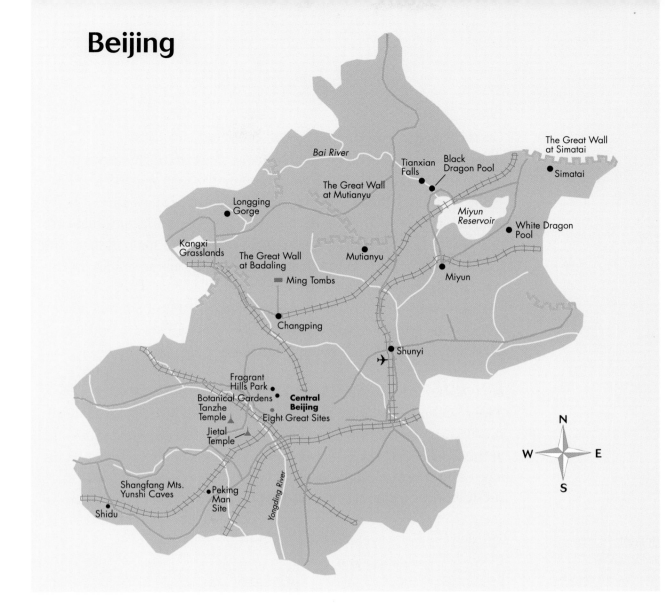

Other historic landmarks noted on the map include the Peking Man Site, located southwest of the central city. Remains of early humans who lived at least 400,000 years ago were found at this site. North-west of the central city, and north of Changping, you'll find 13 imperial tombs belonging to members of China's ruling families from the time of the Ming dynasty (A.D. 1368–1644). West of the central city is Fragrant Hills Park, the hunting ground of early Chinese emperors.

Notice the rail lines running through the map. The large number, and the multiple directions in which they run, suggest the importance of Beijing as a Chinese city.

▲ *Above: Remnants of China's 2,000-year-old Great Wall (marked in a purple zigzag) appear on the northern portion of this map.*

Other Maps and Guides

In addition to road and city street maps, there are many other maps and guides that are useful to us in moving through our world. There are navigational charts for boaters, and maps that show special points of interest, such as all the caves in a state or all the parks or monuments in a city. Floor plans that guide you through famous buildings and museums are another kind of map. And, there are trail guides for hikers, bikers, skiers, and horseback riders.

However you choose to get around our vast and complicated world—and wherever you choose to go—you will always find that maps will help you do it much more easily.

A Travel Map and the Design of a Tomb

The travel map of Hong Kong, below, does not attempt to show all possible transportation routes. It indicates major roads, the route of the Kowloon-Canton Railway, and the location of the airport. This type of information can be valuable in deciding, not only how you might reach your destination, but the best way to explore once you arrive.

▶ **Right:** Hong Kong is made up of all of the land colored green, including the island that is also called Hong Kong.

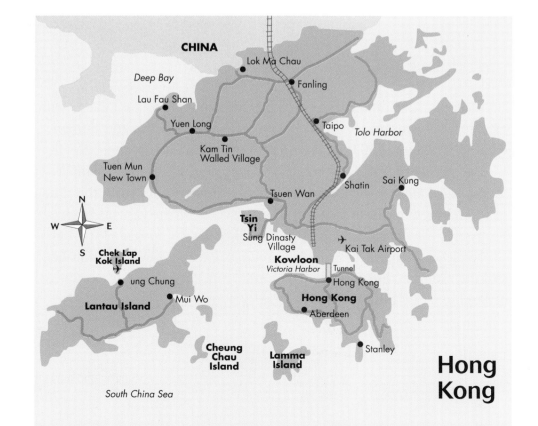

Floor Plan of the Taj Mahal

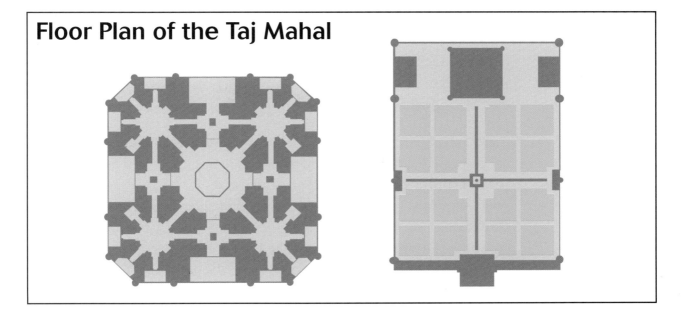

Above is a map of the Taj Mahal. This beautiful, white marble tomb is perhaps the best-known building in India. It was built in the 1600s by one of India's emperors to honor his favorite wife, who died in childbirth. The map offers two views of the Taj Mahal: On the left is the tomb itself. The view on the right shows the tomb in the center and its surrounding grounds. Although you could use these maps to find your way around this landmark, they are not meant to be locator maps. Instead, they simplify the layout of the tomb and grounds to emphasize the elements that went into planning their design. It is easy to see that the design is very symmetrical, or balanced, and that many elements are based on the number four. This was done deliberately: The number four stands for completeness and is a sacred concept in Islam.

▲ *Above:* A plan for the Taj Mahal (left) and its grounds (right) show that this famous landmark has a very well balanced design.

A Closer Look

Sometimes the shape of a road on a map, and even the absence of roads, tells you something about the landscape. Look at the transportation routes map of Asia on page 50. Find areas where there are very few major roads or railroads. Compare this map with the physical map of Asia on page 10 to see if the topography helps explain the way the routes are laid out.

Glossary

acid rain Rain that has collected waste gases from the atmosphere and is damaging to the environment.

cash crop A crop that is grown to be sold.

colonization Occupying another country to use its resources.

Communism A way of organizing a country so that all property and businesses are owned by the government or community and profits are shared by everyone.

deforestation Large-scale clearing of forested land, which may die as a result.

desertification The creation of desert conditions as a result of long droughts, overgrazing, or soil erosion.

drought A long period without rainfall.

erosion Wearing away by the action of wind or water.

export Something sold and shipped to another country.

gross domestic product (GDP) The total output of a country; all products and labor

hardwood Broadleaf trees (see **softwood**).

indigenous Original to a particular place.

ozone layer A layer of gas above Earth's surface that protects it against some of the sun's harmful rays.

per capita Per person (literally, "per head").

plateau A large, mostly level, area of land that is higher than the land surrounding it.

salinization The process by which nutrients are washed from the soil by over-irrigation, leaving the soil encrusted with salts.

shifting agriculture Farming a small area of land until the soil is nearly worn out, then moving on, leaving the first area to grow wild and renew itself naturally.

softwood Coniferous, or cone-bearing, trees.

subsistence farming Growing crops or raising animals for personal use, rather than for sale or trade.

Further Reading

Asia, Australia, New Zealand, and Oceania. Lands and Peoples (series). Danbury, CT: Grolier, Inc., 1997.

Bainey, John. *Japan.* Country Fact Files (series). Austin, TX: Raintree Steck-Vaughn, 1994.

Buettner, Dan. *Sovietrek: A Journey by Bicycle Across Russia.* Minneapolis, MN: Lerner Publications, 1994.

Faneri, Anita. *India.* Country Fact Files (series). Austin, TX: Raintree Steck-Vaughn, 1994.

Flint, David. *Russia.* On the Map (series). New York: Thomson Learning, 1994.

Wright, David K. *Malaysia.* Enchantment of the World (series). Danbury, CT: Children's Press, 1988.

Index

Page numbers for illustrations are in boldface.

DATE DUE			